2011
CAREER
PLAN

The Best Moves Now for a Solid Future

Laurence Shatkin, Ph.D.

JIST Works
America's Career Publisher

2011 CAREER PLAN

© 2011 by JIST Publishing

Published by JIST Works, an imprint of JIST Publishing
7321 Shadeland Station, Suite 200
Indianapolis, Indiana 46256-3923

Phone: 800-648-JIST   Fax: 877-454-7839
E-mail: info@jist.com   Web site: www.jist.com

Some Other Books by Laurence Shatkin, PhD

Best Jobs for the 21st Century	225 Best Jobs for Baby Boomers
200 Best Jobs for College Graduates	250 Best-Paying Jobs
300 Best Jobs Without a Four-Year Degree	150 Best Jobs for a Better World
200 Best Jobs Through Apprenticeships	200 Best Jobs for Introverts
50 Best Jobs for Your Personality	150 Best Recession-Proof Jobs
40 Best Fields for Your Career	

Quantity discounts are available for JIST products. Please call 800-648-JIST or visit www.jist.com for a free catalog and more information.

Visit www.jist.com for information on JIST, free job search information, tables of contents, sample pages, and ordering information on our many products.

Acquisitions Editor: Susan Pines
Development Editor: Stephanie Koutek
Cover Designer: Honeymoon Image & Design, Inc.
Interior Layout: Toi Davis
Proofreaders: Linda Seifert, Jeanne Clark
Indexer: Joy Dean Lee

Printed in the United States of America

15 14 13 12 11 10   9 8 7 6 5 4 3 2 1

Library of Congress Cataloging-in-Publication data is on file with the Library of Congress.

ISBN 978-1-59357-815-2

Make Your Career Plan for 2011

As the U.S. pulls out of recession, 2011 promises more job opportunities than we've seen for several years. Do you have a plan for grabbing those opportunities?

Maybe you want to climb your career ladder. Or start a whole new career. Or just hold on to the job you have now. Whatever you want, you need to *make a plan*. "I'll find *something*" is not a plan.

Opportunities in 2011 will be uneven. Some fields will be growing much faster than others. With this book, you can explore the hottest fields and the hottest jobs in those fields. You'll also identify the gaps in your career plan and get detailed tips for how to bridge those gaps.

So stop dreaming, start acting. Get started on a plan.

Credits and Acknowledgments: While the authors created this book, it is based on the work of many others. The occupational information is based on data obtained from the U.S. Department of Labor and Department of Education. These sources provide the most authoritative occupational information available. The job titles and their related descriptions are from the O*NET database, which was developed by researchers and developers under the direction of the U.S. Department of Labor. They, in turn, were assisted by thousands of employers who provided details on the nature of work in the many thousands of job samplings used in the database's development. We used the most recent version of the O*NET database, release 14.0. We appreciate and thank the staff of the U.S. Department of Labor for their efforts and expertise in providing such a rich source of data.

Table of Contents

PART I

MAKE YOUR PLAN

CHAPTER 1

What 2011 Means for Your Career

Now's the time to get ready for your career move. The one you've been fantasizing about: the move to a better job. Or, if you're unemployed right now, back to work. Not in just any job, but in a *good* job.

America is climbing out of recession now, and job opportunities are better now than they've been for a long time. That's why 2011 is the time to make your move.

It may be a move to a new job, a new occupation, a new industry. Maybe a promotion in your present career path. The nature of the move is for you to decide. But it's time to commit to a move and make a plan.

This book helps you make an action plan. It leads you through a step-by-step process of developing a strategy for your 2011 career move.

This book is not an economics textbook. Nevertheless, I'm going to start by giving you some jargon-free background on the current trends in the working world. That way, you'll understand why 2011 is the right time for you to make your move.

How We Got Here

I don't need to tell you how bad the Great Recession has been. You know people who lost their jobs, even their homes. (Maybe *you* did.) You've probably seen recessions before, like the one that hit 10 years ago when the high-tech bubble burst. But those other economic downturns weren't as severe as this one has been.

In the run-up to the Great Recession, banks made a lot of foolish loans. So did some financial firms that acted like banks but were not required to play by the same rules as banks. And these lenders encouraged a lot of foolish borrowers to take on debt they were not capable of paying off.

To understand what happened to cause the downturn, think of the lending institutions as dancers in a ballroom. Imagine that there are 100 dancers but only 10 chairs. When some of the dancers get tired, they can sit awhile. The ballroom doesn't need 100 chairs as long as the music keeps playing because most of the dancers keep on boogeying instead of sitting down.

But if the music stops, suddenly it's like that game we played in grade school: musical chairs. Everybody in the ballroom runs for a chair, but most of them are out of luck.

For many years, housing prices kept going up and up. People borrowed money to buy homes and then paid it back dependably when they sold their homes for a price well above the purchase price. The rising home prices were music to the ears of the bankers, and they were happy to dance to it.

The lenders doled out money freely to homebuyers. It seemed like a no-lose proposition: Even if a few borrowers failed to meet their payments, the banks could repossess the houses and be confident that the homes had gained in value.

The financial world was like the ballroom: Just as the ballroom let in many more dancers than they had chairs, so the banks and other lending institutions lent out much more money than they actually had in their vaults. They lent it to more and more people, and eventually they were signing up borrowers who lacked enough income to meet their long-term mortgage payments. That seemed fine as long as the music kept playing, as long as housing prices kept going up.

Housing prices actually peaked in early 2005, but it took a couple of years for the dancers to realize that the music had stopped. When people couldn't pay off their home loans, the lending institutions couldn't pay back their investors. They also couldn't get new investors.

I won't go into confusing details about "credit-default swaps" and other seemingly clever maneuvers that these lenders were doing, all of which blew up in their faces. The important concept to take away is that the music was the rising home prices and the dancing was *credit*—the ability of people and businesses to borrow money to finance their activities. Once the music stopped, lenders stopped lending and credit froze up.

The auto dealer couldn't borrow to pay for a new shipment of cars. The company that wanted to build a new corporate headquarters couldn't borrow to pay the construction firm. The manufacturer couldn't borrow to build a new assembly line, and the kinds of products turned out by the old assembly line were being made more cheaply in China. The result: The auto dealer, the construction firm, and the manufacturer all laid off workers. Doing less business, they all paid less in taxes. So did the laid-off workers. That meant the city had to lay off teachers and restaurant inspectors, and the state had to lay off prison guards and road-repair crews. Laid-off workers also did less shopping and dining out. So stores had to lay off sales clerks and buy less from manufacturers, and restaurants had to lay off food servers and buy less from food wholesalers.

Each layoff caused still more layoffs. By the end of 2009, more than five million workers had lost their jobs. Many more were working reduced hours. Still others were staying in unsatisfying jobs, unable to find a better job. (Sound familiar?)

If you were looking for work at that time, I don't have to tell you how dismal the prospects were. But the economy was actually getting ready to turn around.

The Recovery

The greatest loss of jobs in any single month, almost 800,000, happened in January 2009. The next month, job losses were closer to 700,000, and by January 2010 the losses were considerably under 100,000. That was still more jobs lost than gained, though. In fact, the economy needs to *add* a bit more than 100,000 jobs each month just to keep pace with the number of new grads, immigrants, and other people entering the workforce. And it needs a much faster pace of added jobs to create work for the millions idled by the Great Recession.

But as this book goes to press in late 2010, the recovery seems likely to continue and pick up speed. That's why 2011 promises to be a good time to start carrying out your career plan—once you've mapped it out.

Several factors are contributing to this economic upturn. First, most of the banks and other lenders have survived, thanks partly to Washington's bailouts, which started under President Bush and have continued under President Obama. (Yes, these bailouts have added to the national debt. But a recession dragging on for a decade would have added even more.) You may have heard about the government's "stress tests" of the 19 largest lenders, showing that these firms were on sounder footing than many people had believed. With less fear that these lenders would go bankrupt, investors began to pull money out of their mattresses and pump it back into the economy. As credit thaws, as the dancers start moving to the beat, business activity can increase. That means job opportunities for you.

Another boost came from the American Recovery and Reinvestment Act of 2009, usually called the stimulus bill. The stimulus combined tax cuts with funds for road and bridge construction, medical research, student loans, weatherization of old buildings, grants to schools and law enforcement agencies, extension of unemployment benefits, expanded health insurance under Medicaid and COBRA, and many other programs that have created or preserved jobs. Maybe you haven't been hired for one of these jobs, but the people who did have money to spend. Their mortgage payments and investments help keep the lenders dancing, creating more job openings.

The Patient Protection and Affordable Care Act of 2010, usually called the health-care reform bill, also has contributed to the recovery. It expands the number of people who are covered—for example, adult children can stay on their parents' policies until their 27th birthday. It also makes the insurance more affordable—for example, small businesses get a tax credit to offset some of the cost of covering their workers. These changes, plus others that will kick in later, are creating jobs in the already booming health-care field and mean that you won't have to stay in an unsatisfying job for fear of losing health coverage if you leave.

Mass psychology also plays a role in every recovery: After the initial panic caused by bank failures (or near-failures), once people realize that the world hasn't come to an end, they start to spend and invest again—tentatively at first, then with growing confidence. Eventually, the quiet hum of economic activity grows louder. Then people like you can start to plan seriously for a career move.

But this recovery is not a boom, especially for job-seekers. Hiring is on the upswing, but jobs are not expected to be plentiful in 2011—or for several years afterward. We may see a repeat of what happened after the recession of 2001, when 39 months passed before employment rose back to pre-recession levels.

This recovery is also a patchwork affair, with some industries bouncing back much faster than others. For example, by March 2010, while manufacturers were adding jobs, the news and information business was still losing jobs.

That's why "I'll find *something*" is not a career plan for 2011. You need to choose a specific goal and develop a smart strategy to take advantage of the opportunities that 2011 offers. Chapter 3 of this book highlights the fields where the job opportunities are hottest. Part II describes the hottest jobs.

Commit to a 2011 Career Goal

But before you focus on a particular industry or job, you need to identify the *kind of change* you're going to make in your career—for example, changing to a new job or to a new industry. Identify that career goal, and then I'll help you plan how you're going to reach it. Or at least make a start.

Okay, then, what career goal are you *willing to commit to* for 2011? The shape of your 2011 career plan will depend on which goal you choose.

Remember, after you read this book, I don't want you to just nod your head and say, "That's nice to know." I want you to *take action.* And that means having a goal.

The goal doesn't necessarily have to be something you can accomplish fully in 2011. A very ambitious goal may take years to reach. But 2011, with its promise of growing opportunities, is when you should at least make some real progress toward your career goal.

So now let's consider the various types of career goals, ranging from the most modest to the most ambitious. For each type of career goal, I'll show you the outlines of a strategy and which parts of this book will be most useful in planning for that strategy.

GOAL: More security in my present job.

STRATEGY: "Safeguarding"—alignment with company mission; productivity; visibility.

SEE: Chapter 6

GOAL: A promotion in my present job ladder.

STRATEGY: "Climbing"—trial assignment; productivity; visibility.

SEE: Chapters 4, 5, 6

GOAL: A job in my present occupation and in my present industry, but with a new employer.

STRATEGY: "Decamping"—skill tune-up; visibility; networking.

SEE: Chapters 4, 5, 6

GOAL: A job in my present occupation, but with a new employer in a different industry.

STRATEGY: "Revamping"—industry exploration and targeting; skill overhaul; visibility; networking.

SEE: Chapters 2, 4, 5, 6

GOAL: A job with a new employer in a different occupation (maybe your first job).

STRATEGY: "Reinventing"—career exploration and targeting; skill overhaul; visibility; networking.

SEE: Chapters 2, 3, 4, 5, 6

> **Your Assignment:** Circle one of these goals. This is your 2011 career goal.

Key Points: Chapter 1

- The Great Recession was particularly severe because credit froze up, but most lending institutions have recovered.

- As the United States climbs out of recession, 2011 offers many job opportunities.

- Opportunities vary greatly across industries because some are growing much faster than others.

- You need to commit to a 2011 career goal so you can formulate a plan for reaching it (or at least moving toward it).

CHAPTER 2

Take Aim

You're reading this chapter because your 2011 career goal is to move to a new industry or occupation. Or possibly you're planning your first real job. In my terms, you're working up a strategy to either *revamp* or *reinvent* your career.

Let's not kid ourselves, this is a big step. Even before you can start looking for work, you have to choose an industry or occupation that seems like a good fit for you. Out of all the things that people do for a living, how can you make a good choice?

What's Your Personality Type?

Start by considering this: You're not a blank slate. Even if you're a fresh-faced youngster who has never worked full-time, you have preferences—things you like, things you hate. You also have abilities that make you better able to handle some kinds of work than others.

These preferences and abilities add up to make the work-related aspects of your personality. Of course, personality is not the only factor you should consider when you make a career choice. (For example, everybody wants to earn money.) But personality is a good place to start because it provides a big-picture view of the world of work.

The most widely used personality theory about careers was developed by John L. Holland in the early 1950s. The theory rests on the principle that people tend to be happier and more successful in jobs where they feel comfortable with the work tasks and problems, the physical environment, and the kinds of people they work with. Holland identified six personality types that describe basic aspects of work situations. He called them Realistic, Investigative, Artistic, Social, Enterprising, and Conventional. (Some of these labels are difficult to grasp at first glance, but you'll gain a clearer understanding by the time you finish this chapter.) The initials for these personality types spell RIASEC, so that acronym is often used to refer to these types.

Holland argued that most people can be described by one of the RIASEC personality types—the type that dominates—and that likewise each of the various occupations that make up our economy has work situations and settings that match up with one of these personality types. Therefore, if you understand your dominant personality type and then identify which jobs are consistent with that type, you will have a clearer idea of which jobs will suit you best.

Holland recognized that many people and jobs also tend toward a second or third personality type—for example, someone might be described primarily as Conventional and secondarily as Enterprising, and such a person would fit in best working in a job with the CE code, such as Cost Estimators. People like this should also consider jobs coded EC, such as Retail Salespersons, and they might find satisfaction in many jobs with various combinations of codes beginning with either C or E.

Next you're going to do a quick exercise to help you clarify your main personality type or types. At the end of this chapter, you'll see what industries and jobs might be good fits for you.

Keep in mind that personality measurement is not an exact science and this fast checklist is not a scientific instrument. Nevertheless, it should give you insights that will help you understand which kinds of work might suit you best. Use common sense to combine the results of this exercise with other information you can get about yourself and your work options. Talk to people who know you and are familiar with your school and work experiences.

The exercise is easy to do—just follow the directions beginning with Step 1. This is not a test, so there are no right or wrong answers and no time limit.

Step 1: Respond to the Statements

Starting on the next page, carefully read each work activity (items 1 through 120). If you think you would LIKE to do the activity, circle the number of the activity. Don't consider whether you have the education or training needed for it or how much money you might earn if it were part of your job. Simply decide whether you would like the activity. If you know you would dislike the activity or you're not sure, leave the number unmarked.

After you respond to all 120 activities, you'll score your responses in Step 2.

Circle the numbers of the activities you would LIKE to do.

1. Build kitchen cabinets

2. Guard money in an armored car

3. Operate a dairy farm

4. Lay brick or tile

5. Monitor a machine on an assembly line

6. Repair household appliances

7. Drive a taxicab

8. Assemble electronic parts

9. Drive a truck to deliver packages to offices and homes

10. Paint houses

11. Enforce fish and game laws

12. Work on an offshore oil-drilling rig

13. Perform lawn care services

14. Catch fish as a member of a fishing crew

15. Refinish furniture

16. Fix a broken faucet

17. Do cleaning or maintenance work

18. Test the quality of parts before shipment

19. Operate a motorboat to carry passengers

20. Put out forest fires

____ **Page Score for R**

(continued)

(continued)

Circle the numbers of the activities you would LIKE to do.

21. Study the history of past civilizations

22. Study animal behavior

23. Develop a new medicine

24. Study ways to reduce water pollution

25. Determine the infection rate of a new disease

26. Study rocks and minerals

27. Diagnose and treat sick animals

28. Study the personalities of world leaders

29. Study whales and other types of marine life

30. Investigate crimes

31. Study the movement of planets

32. Examine blood samples using a microscope

33. Investigate the cause of a fire

34. Develop psychological profiles of criminals

35. Invent a replacement for sugar

36. Study genetics

37. Study the governments of different countries

38. Do research on plants or animals

39. Do laboratory tests to identify diseases

40. Study weather conditions

____ **Page Score for I**

Circle the numbers of the activities you would LIKE to do.

41. Direct a play

42. Create dance routines for a show

43. Write books or plays

44. Play a musical instrument

45. Write reviews of books or plays

46. Compose or arrange music

47. Act in a movie

48. Dance in a Broadway show

49. Draw pictures

50. Create special effects for movies

51. Conduct a musical choir

52. Audition singers and musicians for a musical show

53. Design sets for plays

54. Announce a radio show

55. Write a song

56. Perform jazz or tap dance

57. Direct a movie

58. Sing in a band

59. Design artwork for magazines

60. Pose for a photographer

____ **Page Score for A**

(continued)

(continued)

Circle the numbers of the activities you would LIKE to do.

61. Perform nursing duties in a hospital

62. Give CPR to someone who has stopped breathing

63. Help people with personal or emotional problems

64. Teach children how to read

65. Work with mentally disabled children

66. Teach an elementary school class

67. Give career guidance to people

68. Supervise the activities of children at a camp

69. Help people with family-related problems

70. Perform rehabilitation therapy

71. Help elderly people with their daily activities

72. Teach children how to play sports

73. Teach sign language to people with hearing disabilities

74. Help people who have problems with drugs or alcohol

75. Help families care for ill relatives

76. Provide massage therapy to people

77. Plan exercises for disabled students

78. Organize activities at a recreational facility

79. Take care of children at a day-care center

80. Teach a high school class

____ **Page Score for S**

Circle the numbers of the activities you would LIKE to do.

81. Buy and sell stocks and bonds

82. Manage a retail store

83. Operate a beauty salon or barbershop

84. Sell merchandise over the telephone

85. Run a stand that sells newspapers and magazines

86. Give a presentation about a product you are selling

87. Sell compact discs at a music store

88. Manage the operations of a hotel

89. Sell houses

90. Manage a supermarket

91. Sell a soft drink product line to stores and restaurants

92. Sell refreshments at a movie theater

93. Sell hair-care products to stores and salons

94. Start your own business

95. Negotiate business contracts

96. Represent a client in a lawsuit

97. Negotiate contracts for professional athletes

98. Market a new line of clothing

99. Sell automobiles

100. Sell computer equipment in a store

____ **Page Score for E**

(continued)

(continued)

Circle the numbers of the activities you would LIKE to do.

101. Develop a spreadsheet using computer software

102. Proofread records or forms

103. Use a computer program to generate customer bills

104. Schedule conferences for an organization

105. Keep accounts payable/receivable for an office

106. Load computer software into a large computer network

107. Organize and schedule office meetings

108. Use a word processor to edit and format documents

109. Direct or transfer phone calls for a large organization

110. Perform office filing tasks

111. Compute and record statistical and other numerical data

112. Take notes during a meeting

113. Calculate the wages of employees

114. Assist senior-level accountants in performing bookkeeping tasks

115. Inventory supplies using a handheld computer

116. Keep records of financial transactions for an organization

117. Record information from customers applying for charge accounts

118. Photocopy letters and reports

119. Stamp, sort, and distribute mail for an organization

120. Handle customers' bank transactions

____ **Page Score for C**

Step 2: Score Your Responses

Do the following to score your responses:

1. Score the responses on each page. On each page of responses, go from top to bottom and count how many numbers are circled. Then write that total on the "Page Score" line at the bottom of the page. Go on to the next page and do the same there.

2. Determine your primary interest area. Which Page Score has your highest score: **R, I, A, S, E,** or **C**? Enter the letter for that personality type on the following line.

My Primary Personality Type: ____

You will use your Primary Personality Type *first* to explore careers. (If two Page Scores are tied for the highest scores or are within 4 points of each other, use both of them for your Primary Personality Type. You are equally divided between two types.)

R=Realistic. Realistic personalities like work activities that include practical, hands-on problems and solutions. They enjoy dealing with plants; animals; and real-world materials such as wood, tools, and machinery. They enjoy outside work. Often they do not like occupations that mainly involve doing paperwork or working closely with others.

I=Investigative. Investigative personalities like work activities that have to do with ideas and thinking more than with physical activity. They like to search for facts and figure out problems mentally rather than to persuade or lead people.

A=Artistic. Artistic personalities like work activities that deal with the artistic side of things, such as forms, designs, and patterns. They like self-expression in their work. They prefer settings where work can be done without following a clear set of rules.

S=Social. Social personalities like work activities that assist others and promote learning and personal development. They prefer to communicate more than to work with objects, machines, or data. They like to teach, to give advice, to help, or otherwise to be of service to people.

E=Enterprising. Enterprising personalities like work activities having to do with starting up and carrying out projects, especially business ventures. They like persuading and leading people and making decisions. They like taking risks for profit. These personalities prefer action rather than thought.

C=Conventional. Conventional personalities like work activities that follow set procedures and routines. They prefer working with data and details rather than with ideas. They prefer work in which there are precise standards rather than work in which you have to judge things by yourself. These personalities like working where the lines of authority are clear.

3. Determine your secondary interest areas. Which Page Score has your next highest score? Which has your third highest score? Enter the letters for those areas here.

My Secondary Personality Types: ___ ___

(If you do not find many industries or occupations that you like using your Primary Personality Type, you can use your Secondary Personality Types to look at more career options.)

Step 3: Find Industries That Suit Your Personality Type

(You can skip this step if you already know what industry you want to aim for—maybe the one you're working in now.)

Use the following table to find one or more industries that suit your personality type or interest you. Write the industry name or names in the blanks at the end of this chapter, and then turn to chapter 3 to read about opportunities in those fields.

If you want to find industries that *combine* your Primary Personality Type and a Secondary Personality Type, look for industries listed for *both* of these RIASEC types.

Realistic	Construction; Employment Services
Investigative	Child Day Care Services; Computer Systems Design and Related Services; Construction; Educational Services; Employment Services; Health Care; Management, Scientific, and Technical Consulting Services; Scientific Research and Development Services; Social Assistance, Except Child Day Care; Software Publishers

Artistic	Advocacy, Grantmaking, and Civic Organizations; Child Day Care Services; Computer Systems Design and Related Services; Construction; Educational Services; Health Care; Scientific Research and Development Services; Social Assistance, Except Child Day Care; Software Publishers
Social	Advocacy, Grantmaking, and Civic Organizations; Child Day Care Services; Educational Services; Health Care; Social Assistance, Except Child Day Care
Enterprising	Advocacy, Grantmaking, and Civic Organizations; Management, Scientific, and Technical Consulting Services
Conventional	Computer Systems Design and Related Services; Employment Services; Management, Scientific, and Technical Consulting Services; Scientific Research and Development Services; Software Publishers

When exploring industries, you should be especially careful to consider secondary personality types as well as the primary type. That's because even an industry that is dominated by a certain personality type has niches where other types can be happily employed.

Step 4: Find Jobs That Suit Your Personality Type

Start with your Primary Personality Type and find matching jobs in the following table, which is organized according to the six personality types ("RIASEC"). When you find a job that interests you, write the name in one of the blanks at the end of this chapter. Then turn to Part II and read the job description for that job. Don't rule out a job just because the title is not familiar to you.

If you want to find jobs that *combine* your Primary Personality Type and a Secondary Personality Type, look in the following table for RIASEC codes that match the two codes in either order. For example, if your Primary Personality Type is Investigative and your Secondary Personality Type is

Realistic, you would look for jobs in the table coded IR. You will also find jobs coded IR_, and you'll find still more jobs coded I_R. All of these jobs are worth considering. Finally, to cast an even wider net, you may want to consider reversing the codes you're looking for. Keep in mind that these jobs may not be quite as satisfying because your Primary Personality Type, though represented, does not dominate.

If your Primary Personality Type is Artistic, you certainly will want to look beyond the first letter of the codes in the table, because only one job is listed with a code that begins with A. Why so few jobs that are primarily Artistic? This book is about careers with lots of job opportunities, and careers in the arts are always highly competitive. Nevertheless, you'll find many jobs here with Artistic as a Secondary Personality Type, such as teaching jobs that are primarily Social.

Occupation Name	RIASEC Code(s)
Realistic	
Septic Tank Servicers and Sewer Pipe Cleaners	R
Electrical and Electronics Repairers, Commercial and Industrial Equipment	RIC
Industrial Machinery Mechanics	RIC
Telecommunications Equipment Installers and Repairers, Except Line Installers	RIC
Construction Laborers	RC
Heating, Air Conditioning, and Refrigeration Mechanics and Installers	RC
Security and Fire Alarm Systems Installers	RC
Computer Support Specialists	RCI
Maintenance and Repair Workers, General	RCI
Investigative	
Biomedical Engineers	IR
Medical Scientists, Except Epidemiologists	IRA
Computer Software Engineers, Applications	IRC
Mechanical Engineers	IRC
Biochemists and Biophysicists	IAR
Optometrists	ISR

Physician Assistants	ISR
Market Research Analysts	IEC
Network Systems and Data Communications Analysts	IC
Computer Software Engineers, Systems Software	ICR
Network and Computer Systems Administrators	ICR
Industrial Engineers	ICE
Survey Researchers	ICE

Artistic

Editors	AEC

Social

Home Health Aides	SR
Physical Therapist Aides	SR
Physical Therapist Assistants	SRI
Coaches and Scouts	SRE
Dental Hygienists	SRC
Medical and Public Health Social Workers	SI
Occupational Therapists	SI
Rehabilitation Counselors	SI
Physical Therapists	SIR
Speech-Language Pathologists	SIA
Instructional Coordinators	SIE
Kindergarten Teachers, Except Special Education	SA
Preschool Teachers, Except Special Education	SA
Special Education Teachers, Preschool, Kindergarten, and Elementary School	SA
Self-Enrichment Education Teachers	SAE
Training and Development Specialists	SAC
Child, Family, and School Social Workers	SE
Health Educators	SE
Education Administrators, Preschool and Child Care Center/Program	SEC
Medical Assistants	SCR

(continued)

(continued)

Enterprising

Police and Sheriff's Patrol Officers	ERS
Public Relations Specialists	EAS
Employment, Recruitment, and Placement Specialists	ESC
Loan Counselors	ESC
Logisticians	EC
Retail Salespersons	EC
Sales Representatives, Wholesale and Manufacturing, Technical and Scientific Products	EC
Computer and Information Systems Managers	ECI
Customer Service Representatives	ECS
First-Line Supervisors/Managers of Personal Service Workers	ECS
General and Operations Managers	ECS

Conventional

Dental Assistants	CRS
Database Administrators	CI
Financial Analysts	CIE
Computer Systems Analysts	CIR
Social and Human Service Assistants	CSE
Compensation, Benefits, and Job Analysis Specialists	CE
Cost Estimators	CE
Production, Planning, and Expediting Clerks	CE
Purchasing Agents, Except Wholesale, Retail, and Farm Products	CE
Office Clerks, General	CER
Accountants and Auditors	CEI
Compliance Officers, Except Agriculture, Construction, Health and Safety, and Transportation	CEI

Commit to Exploring an Industry or Job

Let me remind you once again that this book is about *taking action* in 2011. Your next action should be to inform yourself about industries or jobs that might be a good fit for your personality. Get started right now by committing yourself to explore one or more titles from the tables in this chapter.

Write in the industries or jobs here:

_____

_____

_____

Now turn to chapter 3 to learn more about an industry or Part II to learn more about a job.

Key Points: Chapter 2

- A useful way to narrow down your options is by identifying the industries and jobs that are a good fit for your personality.

- Your personality may be described by one, two, or even three types.

The Hottest Fields of 2011

As the economy heats up, it doesn't work like an oven that browns all the biscuits at the same rate. Some industries are much hotter than others. So it makes sense for you to focus your 2011 career plan on a field that is expected to offer lots of job opportunities.

In this chapter, you're going to look at 11 high-opportunity fields that have been identified by the U.S. Department of Labor. You'll learn what the major trends are in each field, plus the names of the hottest jobs. (You can read important facts about these jobs in Part II.)

Which field is right for you? That depends on several considerations:

- **Personal preferences.** The exercise you did in chapter 2 suggested some fields that might suit your personality. Pay special attention to these fields. But keep in mind that there are jobs in every field that don't conform to the dominant personality types in that field.

- **Your work experience.** You may want to give priority to a field because you have already have worked in it. (Maybe you're working there *now*.) Having your foot in the door can be a big advantage in your 2011 career move. On the other hand, your experiences in the field may have convinced you to get out. Either way, your insider's knowledge can help with your decision.

- **Your background of education or training.** Maybe one or more of the hot fields aligns well with a college degree you hold or with a formal training program you've completed. You'd be wise to craft a 2011 career plan that takes advantage of credentials you already hold (or will soon).

- **Local opportunities.** It's likely that some of these fields employ many workers in your community or in locations close enough for you to commute to. On the other hand, maybe you can rule out some fields because of a *lack* of local employers (unless you're willing to relocate).

- **Personal connections.** You may favor a field because you know somebody who works in it or in a closely related field. That person can advise you about the best opportunities—and maybe even connect you to a job opening.

In fact, any one of these considerations may cause you to reject all 11 of the fields covered here and look for work in some *other* fields instead. The truth is, these 11 fields *are not the only fields* where you can find job opportunities in 2011. They're fast-growing, but jobs can be found in many fields that are not growing as fast—even shrinking.

For example, the utilities industry is expected to shrink by 10.8 percent, but it will offer excellent job prospects for qualified applicants. How can that be? In 2008, about 53 percent of the utilities workforce was age 45 or older. Because this field uses on-the-job training for many occupations, it will need to recruit many new workers so they will be fully trained when the large cohort of older workers retires.

Similar opportunities are available in other fields and in specialized niches within almost every field. To learn about other fields, see the note at the end of this chapter about where to get more information about various fields.

Eleven Hot Fields and Their Hottest Jobs

The 11 hot fields described here are ordered by the amount of growth projected for them between 2008 and 2018, with the fastest-growing listed first. For each field, you'll see the following information:

- **What the Field Does**—a brief explanation of the needs the field serves and how the field is divided into various kinds of companies.

- **Employment**—what the working conditions are like and whether employers are typically large or small.

- **Getting Started**—the most common entry requirements for the field.

- **Job Prospects**—where the best job opportunities in the field may be found.

- **Hottest Jobs**—a list of the fastest-growing occupations in the field, with industry-specific facts about occupational growth, workforce size, and average earnings.

Each list of the hottest jobs, like the fields in this chapter, is ordered by the jobs' rates of growth. Of the 65 unique occupations listed, all are growing by at least 11.9 percent (and often much faster) *within their field* over the 2008–2018 time period. All pay an average of more than $21,720 per year within their field, which is a level of pay better than what one-quarter of wage-earning Americans are earning. In addition, they all account for at least 5,000 workers within their field (except in a couple of very large fields, where the minimum is even higher); this is important to know, because even a fast-growing occupation will not create many job openings if it is small to begin with.

Let me emphasize that the economic figures you'll see for the occupations apply only *within the field* being discussed. Opportunities for the same occupations may be much less rosy in other fields. For example, employment of General and Operations Managers in the software publishing field is expected to grow by 16.5 percent, and their average earnings in that field came to an impressive $134,010. Throughout the whole economy, however, this same occupation is actually expected to *shrink* slightly, and its average pay across all industries is almost one-third lower, $91,570. In some industries this occupation is shrinking severely; the telecommunications field, for example, will shed about 20 percent of these workers.

That's why your 2011 career plan needs to focus on the hot industries rather than just looking at occupations.

All of these hot jobs are described in Part II of this book. So when you see a job that looks interesting, circle it. That will help you remember to look it up in Part II.

Management, Scientific, and Technical Consulting Services

What the Field Does. Firms that offer management, scientific, and technical consulting services influence how businesses, governments, and institutions make decisions. Often working behind the scenes, these firms offer technical expertise, information, contacts, and tools that clients cannot provide themselves. They then work with their clients to provide a service or solve a problem.

Usually, one of the resources that consulting firms provide to clients is expertise—in the form of knowledge, experience, special skills, or creativity; another resource is time or personnel that the client cannot spare. Clients include large and small companies in the private sector; federal, state, and local government agencies; institutions, such as hospitals, universities, unions, and nonprofit organizations; and foreign governments or businesses.

The management, scientific, and technical consulting services industry is diverse. Almost anyone with expertise in a given area can enter consulting, which means that it can be a good field to move into after you have acquired a lot of skills and knowledge in some other industry.

Management consulting firms advise on almost every aspect of corporate operations, and scientific and technical consulting firms provide technical advice relating to almost all nonmanagement organizational activities.

Larger consulting firms usually provide expertise in a variety of areas, whereas smaller consulting firms generally specialize in one area of consulting. If you have a proven track record of skills and productivity, or if you're a new graduate with an impressive education, you can probably identify a consulting firm that hires people in your specialization.

Businesses like to hire consultants because these experts are experienced; are well trained; and keep abreast of the latest technologies, government regulations, and management and production techniques. In addition, consultants are cost effective, because they can be hired temporarily and can perform their duties objectively, free of the influence of company politics.

Employment. Consultants work slightly longer hours than most other workers, and occasionally they work evenings or weekends under stress to meet hurried deadlines. Consultants whose services are billed hourly often are under pressure to manage their time very carefully.

Although the vast majority of consulting firms are fairly small, employing fewer than five workers, large firms tend to dominate the job opportunities. Approximately 41 percent of jobs are found in establishments with 50 or more employees, and some of the largest firms in the industry employ several thousand people.

Some occupations, such as environmental engineers, consult primarily with businesses in only one industry, but most of the fastest-growing occupations consult with businesses in diverse industries.

Getting Started. Workers enter this industry via a wide variety of routes. Although employers generally prefer a bachelor's or higher degree, most jobs also require extensive on-the-job training or related experience. Advancement opportunities are best for workers with the highest levels of education.

Some consultants start their own firm as a self-employed, one-person operation, eventually taking on a small support staff.

Job Prospects. Despite the impressive growth projected for this industry, there will be keen competition for jobs because of the prestigious and independent nature of the work and the generous salary and benefits. With more job seekers than openings every year, the best job prospects will probably be for individuals with the most education and work experience.

Hottest Jobs. Employment in this field is projected to grow by 82.7 percent from 2008 to 2018. All of the following occupations are projected to grow within this industry by at least 85.5 percent. Note that the following facts about these occupations apply only to workers *within this industry*. For more generalized information about these occupations, see Part II.

Hottest Jobs in Management, Scientific, and Technical Consulting Services

Occupation	Occupational Growth Within Industry	Workforce Size Within Industry	Average Earnings Within Industry
1. Network Systems and Data Communications Analysts	148.2%	6,560	$74,410
2. Industrial Engineers	111.8%	5,070	$82,440
3. Financial Analysts	104.1%	9,120	$74,380
4. Customer Service Representatives	104.0%	27,980	$31,520
5. Public Relations Specialists	104.0%	8,350	$57,530
6. Training and Development Specialists	103.9%	6,640	$60,420
7. Computer Software Engineers, Applications	102.4%	11,660	$89,190
8. Computer Software Engineers, Systems Software	102.4%	11,420	$94,170
9. Compensation, Benefits, and Job Analysis Specialists	102.1%	5,200	$60,340

Computer Systems Design and Related Services

What the Field Does. Virtually all organizations rely on computer and information technology to conduct business and operate efficiently. Many institutions, however, do not have the internal resources to effectively design, implement, or manage the computer products and systems that they need. When faced with such limitations, organizations often turn to the computer systems design and related services industry.

Establishments in this industry design computer and information systems, develop custom software programs, and manage computer facilities. They also may perform various other functions, such as software installation and disaster recovery. They generally work on a contract basis, assisting an organization with a particular project or problem, such as setting up a secure Web site or establishing a marketplace online, or for ongoing activities, such as the management of an onsite data center or help desk.

The widespread use of the Internet and intranets has resulted in an increased focus on information security. In response, many organizations are employing the services of security consulting firms, which specialize in all aspects of information technology (IT) security. These firms assess computer systems for areas of vulnerability, manage firewalls, and provide protection against intrusion and software viruses.

The technology allows some work to be done from remote locations by means of e-mail and the Internet. For example, systems analysts may work from home with their computers linked directly to computers at the location of their employer or client. Computer support specialists, likewise, can tap into a customer's computer remotely to identify and fix problems.

Employment. Although about 78 percent of establishments in this field employed fewer than 5 workers in 2008, most jobs are found in establishments that employ 50 or more workers.

Computer specialists make up the majority of professional and related occupations, accounting for about 55 percent of the industry as a whole. Their duties vary by occupation and include such tasks as developing computer software, designing information systems, and maintaining network security. Managers direct the work of these specialists, often after a background of working in a computer specialization. Partly because of the expanding use of e-commerce, a substantial number of workers in this field are employed in sales and related occupations. Others work in marketing and sales or improve the presentation and features of Web sites and other Web-related content.

Getting Started. Occupations in this field require varying levels of education, but because of the high proportion of workers in professional occupations, the education level of workers in this industry is higher than average. The kind of training required can change as employers' needs change—for example, the growing interest in computer security. It often is helpful to have skill and expertise in other fields besides computers. Computer software engineers who develop e-commerce applications, for example, should have some expertise in sales or finance.

Job Prospects. Given the rate at which this industry is expected to grow, job opportunities should be excellent for most workers. The best opportunities will be in computer specialist occupations, reflecting their growth and the continuing demand for the high-level skills that are needed to keep up with changes in technology. In addition, as individuals and organizations continue to conduct business electronically, the importance of maintaining system and network security will increase. Employment opportunities should be especially good for individuals involved in cyberspace security services, such as disaster recovery services, custom security programming, and security software installation services.

Hottest Jobs. Employment in this field is projected to grow by 45.3 percent from 2008 to 2018. All of the following occupations are projected to grow within this industry by at least 54.3 percent. Note that the following facts about these occupations apply only to workers *within this industry*. For more generalized information about these occupations, see Part II.

Hottest Jobs in Computer Systems Design and Related Services

Occupation	Occupational Growth Within Industry	Workforce Size Within Industry	Average Earnings Within Industry
1. Network Systems and Data Communications Analysts	95.6%	41,350	$73,440
2. Network and Computer Systems Administrators	71.7%	50,500	$72,190
3. Accountants and Auditors	65.5%	18,540	$67,450
4. Computer Software Engineers, Systems Software	57.4%	113,710	$91,310
5. Computer Support Specialists	57.4%	99,820	$44,030
6. Computer Software Engineers, Applications	57.3%	175,160	$86,510
7. Database Administrators	57.3%	18,820	$78,500
8. Employment, Recruitment, and Placement Specialists	54.4%	8,480	$58,580

Occupation	Occupational Growth Within Industry	Workforce Size Within Industry	Average Earnings Within Industry
9. Purchasing Agents, Except Wholesale, Retail, and Farm Products	54.3%	5,060	$62,400
10. Training and Development Specialists	54.3%	7,180	$59,610

Social Assistance, Except Child Day Care

What the Field Does. At times, people need help to live a full and productive life. They may need assistance finding a job or appropriate child care, learning skills to find employment, locating safe and adequate housing, or getting nutritious food for their family. The social assistance industry provides help to individuals and families to aid them in becoming healthy and productive members of society.

Social assistance establishments provide a wide array of services that include helping the homeless, counseling troubled individuals, training the unemployed or underemployed, and helping families obtain financial assistance. In general, organizations in this industry work to improve the lives of the individuals and families they serve and to enrich their communities. The specific services provided vary greatly, depending on the population the establishment is trying to serve and its goals or mission.

Establishments in the individual and family services sector work to provide the skills and resources necessary for individuals to be more self-sufficient and for families to live in a stable and safe environment. Many of the services in this sector are aimed at a particular population, such as children, the elderly, or those with mental or physical disabilities.

Another sector of this field provides community food services, community housing services, and emergency and other relief services.

Still another sector, vocational rehabilitation services, helps people who are disabled, either from birth or as a result of an illness or injury. The workers teach clients the skills necessary to live independently and to find employment. These workers may also provide job counseling and assist in locating training and educational programs.

Employment. Some social assistance establishments operate around the clock, and evening, weekend, and holiday work is common. Some establishments may be understaffed, resulting in large caseloads for each worker. Jobs in voluntary, nonprofit agencies often are part time.

Careers in social assistance appeal to people with a strong desire to make life better and easier for others. Workers in this industry are usually good communicators and enjoy interacting with people.

Getting Started. Training requirements within this industry vary greatly based on occupation, state licensure requirements, and the setting in which the work is done. Many workers begin in this industry by working as a volunteer. However, for many occupations, a bachelor's or master's degree is required for entrance into the industry.

Job Prospects. Besides job openings arising from employment growth, many additional openings will stem from the need to replace workers who transfer to other occupations or stop working. Workers leave jobs in this industry at a higher rate than the rest of the economy, making job prospects excellent.

Hottest Jobs. Employment in this field is projected to grow by 42.8 percent from 2008 to 2018. All of the following occupations are projected to grow within this industry by at least 31.7 percent. Note that the following facts about these occupations apply only to workers *within this industry.* For more generalized information about these occupations, see Part II.

Hottest Jobs in Social Assistance, Except Child Day Care

Occupation	Occupational Growth Within Industry	Workforce Size Within Industry	Average Earnings Within Industry
1. Medical and Public Health Social Workers	58.0%	47,810	$37,927
2. Special Education Teachers, Preschool, Kindergarten, and Elementary School	56.8%	10,530	$42,580
3. First-Line Supervisors/Managers of Personal Service Workers	51.0%	33,010	$32,942
4. Occupational Therapists	46.0%	16,120	$53,061
5. Social and Human Service Assistants	44.8%	311,810	$26,284
6. Speech-Language Pathologists	43.4%	6,860	$63,238
7. Training and Development Specialists	36.2%	26,020	$37,597
8. Customer Service Representatives	35.9%	8,000	$29,017
9. Public Relations Specialists	34.3%	19,190	$41,930
10. Rehabilitation Counselors	31.7%	159,950	$28,807

Software Publishers

What the Field Does. Software publishing establishments are involved in all aspects of producing and distributing computer software, such as designing, providing documentation, assisting in installation, and providing support services to customers. Unlike print publishers, software publishers usually distribute their products as CD-ROMs, as software preloaded on new computers, or as downloads over the Internet. Some establishments in this industry design, develop, and publish software and others publish only.

Software is often divided into two main categories—applications software and systems software. *Applications software* includes individual programs for computer users—such as word processing and spreadsheet packages, games and graphics packages, data storage programs, and Web browsing programs. *Systems software,* on the other hand, includes operating systems and all of the related programs that enable computers to function. Establishments that design and publish prepackaged software may specialize in one of these areas or may be involved in both. Some establishments also may install software on a customer's system and provide user support.

Much of the applications and system software that is now developed is intended for use on the Internet and for connections to the Internet. Widespread use of the Internet and intranets also has led to a demand for security software, such as firewalls and antivirus applications, to protect computer networks or individual computer environments. Another recent trend is offering software services over the Internet (usually called "cloud computing"). While online e-mail and data storage have been offered for several years, word processing, spreadsheet, and other services are increasingly moving to the World Wide Web.

Employment. Workers in this field put in slightly longer hours than most other workers. Some are able to work at home, using e-mail and Internet network connections.

Although the industry has both large and small firms, the average establishment in software publishing is relatively small; about 62 percent of the establishments employed fewer than five workers in 2008. Many of these small establishments are startup firms that hope to capitalize on a market niche. About 77 percent of jobs, however, are found in establishments that employ 50 or more workers.

Computer specialists make up the vast majority of professional and related occupations among software publishers, accounting for about 52 percent of the industry as a whole. A substantial number of marketing and sales workers also are employed in this field, promoting and selling the products and services produced by the industry.

Getting Started. Occupations in the software publishing industry require varying levels of education, but because of the large number of workers in professional occupations, the education level of workers in this industry is higher than average.

Workers who do programming and engineering typically have a bachelor's or higher degree, in addition to broad knowledge and experience with computer systems and technologies. Workers in computer support, marketing, and sales generally need less formal education.

Job Prospects. Job opportunities in software publishing should be excellent for most workers, given the rate at which the industry is expected to grow, together with the increasing integration and application of software into all sectors of the economy. Computer specialists should enjoy the best opportunities, reflecting continuing demand for workers with high-level skills to keep up with changes in technology.

Hottest Jobs. Employment in this field is projected to grow by 30.1 percent from 2008 to 2018. All of the occupations on the list are projected to grow within this industry by at least 16.5 percent. Note that the following facts about these occupations apply only to workers *within this industry.* For more generalized information about these occupations, see Part II.

Hottest Jobs in Software Publishers

Occupation	Occupational Growth Within Industry	Workforce Size Within Industry	Average Earnings Within Industry
1. Network and Computer Systems Administrators	55.2%	6,670	$80,520
2. Computer Systems Analysts	42.3%	11,440	$80,590
3. Computer Support Specialists	42.2%	18,930	$47,420
4. Market Research Analysts	41.2%	6,070	$98,380
5. Customer Service Representatives	41.2%	6,970	$33,500
6. Computer and Information Systems Managers	30.3%	9,320	$128,960
7. Computer Software Engineers, Applications	29.3%	39,070	$89,840

Occupation	Occupational Growth Within Industry	Workforce Size Within Industry	Average Earnings Within Industry
8. Computer Software Engineers, Systems Software	29.3%	26,080	$95,610
9. Sales Representatives, Wholesale and Manufacturing, Technical and Scientific Products	28.3%	10,100	$77,850
10. General and Operations Managers	16.5%	5,510	$130,850

Scientific Research and Development Services

What the Field Does. From carbon nanotubes to vaccines, workers in the scientific research and development services industry today create the technologies that will change the way people live and work in the future. New technologies can quickly revolutionize business and leisure, as the Internet has.

Research and development (R&D) comprises three types of activity: basic research, applied research, and development. *Basic research* is conducted to advance scientific knowledge without any direct application. This sort of research typically involves a high level of theory and is very risky; many projects fail to produce useful or novel results. Because of this risk, and because it is difficult to determine in advance what new products will result, most basic research is funded by government, universities, or nonprofit organizations. *Applied research* is the bridge between science and business. It is directed toward solving some general problem, but may produce several viable options that all achieve some aspect of the goal. *Development,* which accounts for more than half of all R&D spending, according to the National Science Board, then refines the technologies or processes of applied research into immediately usable products. Most development is done by private industry and is generally oriented toward manufacturing.

The industry includes several sectors, defined by the kind of science and practical applications they focus on. For example, some fast-growing sectors are biotechnology and nanotechnology (which concerns structures as small as molecules). Other important sectors conduct research and development related to consumer products such as automobiles, aircraft, pharmaceuticals, and electronics.

Employment. Most workers in this industry work in offices or laboratories; the location and hours of work vary greatly, however, depending on the requirements of each project. Experiments may run at odd hours, require constant observation, or depend on external conditions such as the weather. In some fields, research or testing must be done in harsh environments to ensure the usefulness of the final product in a wide range of environments. Other research, particularly biomedical research, is conducted in hospitals. Workers in product development may spend much time building proto-types in workshops or laboratories, while research design typically takes place in offices.

Although scientific research and development services can be found in many places, the industry is concentrated in a few areas. Just seven states—California, New York, Massachusetts, Illinois, Maryland, Pennsylvania, and New Jersey—account for more than half of all employment in the industry. There are many small establishments in this field, but 55 percent of employment was in establishments with more than 250 workers in 2008.

Getting Started. Scientific research and development services rely heavily on workers with extensive postsecondary education. A larger percentage of workers in this industry have bachelor's or graduate level degrees than in all other industries.

For most science and engineering occupations, a bachelor's degree is generally the minimal level of education, and a master's or Ph.D. degree is typically necessary for senior researchers. Some fields require a Ph.D. even for entry-level research positions, particularly in basic research. Continuing training is necessary for workers to keep pace with current developments in their fields. It may take the form of on-the-job training or formal training, or it may consist of attending conferences or meetings of professional societies. Workers who fail to remain up to date in their field and related disciplines may face unfavorable job prospects if interest in their current area of expertise declines.

As scientists or engineers gain expertise in a particular field of R&D, they may advance to more senior research positions or become managers. Those who remain in technical positions may undertake more creative work, designing research or developing new technologies at a higher level.

Self-employment is uncommon in scientific research and development services because of the high cost of equipment, but opportunities to start small companies do exist. These opportunities are particularly prevalent in rapidly growing fields, partly due to the availability of investment capital. Self-employed workers in scientific R&D typically have advanced degrees and have worked in academia or other research facilities and form companies to develop commercial products resulting from prior basic or applied research.

Workers in business support occupations, such as accountants and market research analysts, typically have a bachelor's degree in their business specialization.

Job Prospects. Overall prospects for scientists and engineers should be favorable, with better opportunities for scientists who have doctoral degrees, which prepare graduates for research. However, competition for basic and applied research funding is expected in all fields. Creativity is crucial, because scientists and engineers engaged in R&D are expected to propose new research or designs. Experienced scientists and engineers also must remain current and adapt to changes in technologies that may shift interest—and employment—from one area of research to another.

Most R&D programs have long project cycles that continue during economic downturns. However, funding of R&D, particularly by private industry, is closely scrutinized during these periods. Because the federal government provides a significant portion of all R&D funding, shifts in policy also can have a marked impact on employment opportunities, particularly in basic research and aerospace.

Hottest Jobs. Employment in this field is projected to grow by 25.4 percent from 2008 to 2018. All of the following occupations are projected to grow within this industry by at least 37.2 percent. Note that the following facts about these occupations apply only to workers *within this industry*. For more generalized information about these occupations, see Part II.

Hottest Jobs in Scientific Research and Development Services

Occupation	Occupational Growth Within Industry	Workforce Size Within Industry	Average Earnings Within Industry
1. Biomedical Engineers	90.4%	5,720	$82,400
2. Network Systems and Data Communications Analysts	67.4%	7,720	$80,330
3. Biochemists and Biophysicists	50.6%	20,160	$86,430
4. Medical Scientists, Except Epidemiologists	50.0%	68,760	$81,320

(continued)

(continued)

Occupation	Occupational Growth Within Industry	Workforce Size Within Industry	Average Earnings Within Industry
5. Compliance Officers, Except Agriculture, Construction, Health and Safety, and Transportation	49.9%	5,230	$70,770
6. Industrial Engineers	44.4%	17,220	$84,660
7. Survey Researchers	43.1%	7,260	$58,310
8. Computer Software Engineers, Systems Software	37.8%	40,840	$102,040
9. Computer Software Engineers, Applications	37.7%	26,200	$92,580
10. Purchasing Agents, Except Wholesale, Retail, and Farm Products	37.2%	10,280	$67,030

Health Care

What the Field Does. Combining medical technology and the human touch, the health-care industry diagnoses, treats, and administers care around the clock, responding to the needs of millions of people—from newborns to the terminally ill. The workers range from professionals who make life-or-death decisions to office assistants who handle billing, appointment scheduling, and medical records.

Technological advances have made many new procedures and methods of diagnosis and treatment possible. Clinical developments, such as infection control, less invasive surgical techniques, advances in reproductive technology, and gene therapy for cancer treatment, continue to increase the longevity and improve the quality of life of many Americans. Advances in medical technology also have improved the survival rates of trauma victims and the severely ill, who need extensive care from therapists and social workers as well as other support personnel. In addition, advances in information technology have a perceived improvement on patient care and worker efficiency.

Cost containment also is shaping the health-care industry, as shown by the growing emphasis on providing services on an outpatient, ambulatory basis; limiting unnecessary or low-priority services; and stressing preventive care, which reduces the potential cost of undiagnosed, untreated medical conditions. Enrollment in managed care programs continues to grow.

These prepaid plans provide comprehensive coverage to members and control health insurance costs by emphasizing preventive care.

The recently passed legislation reforming health insurance will increase the number of people who are covered, which in turn increases the number of people being treated by health-care providers and the number and type of health-care procedures that will be performed.

Employment. About 76 percent of health-care establishments are offices of physicians, dentists, or other health practitioners. Although hospitals constitute only 1 percent of all health-care establishments, they employ 35 percent of all workers.

Many workers in the health-care industry are on part-time schedules. Many health-care establishments operate around the clock and need staff at all hours, so shift work is common in some occupations, such as registered nurses. It is not uncommon for health-care workers hold more than one part-time job.

Health-care workers involved in direct patient care must take precautions to prevent back strain from lifting patients and equipment; to minimize exposure to radiation and caustic chemicals; and to guard against infectious diseases.

Getting Started. A wide variety of people with various educational backgrounds are necessary for the health-care industry to function. The health-care industry employs some highly educated occupations that require many years of training beyond graduate school. However, most of the occupations in this field require less than four years of college.

A variety of postsecondary programs provide specialized training for jobs in health care. People interested in a career as a health diagnosing and treating practitioner—such as physicians and surgeons, optometrists, physical therapists, or audiologists—should be prepared to complete graduate school coupled with many years of education and training beyond college. A bachelor's degree is required for a few health-care workers, such as health service managers and some RNs. A majority of the technologist and technician occupations require a certificate or an associate degree; these programs usually have both classroom and clinical instruction and last about two years.

The health-care industry also provides many job opportunities for people without specialized training beyond high school. In fact, 47 percent of workers in nursing and residential care facilities have a high school diploma or less, as do 20 percent of workers in hospitals.

Persons considering careers in health care should have a strong desire to help others, genuine concern for the welfare of patients and clients, and an ability to deal with people of diverse backgrounds in stressful situations. Many of the health-care jobs that are regulated by state licensure require health-care professionals to complete continuing education at regular intervals to maintain valid licensure.

Job Prospects. Many job openings should arise in all employment settings as a result of employment growth and the need to replace workers who retire or leave their jobs for other reasons.

Occupations with the most replacement openings are usually large, with high turnover stemming from low pay and status, poor benefits, low training requirements, and a high proportion of young and part-time workers. Nursing aides, orderlies and attendants, and home health aides are among the occupations adding the most new jobs in this industry between 2008 and 2018, about 592,200 combined.

Another occupation that is expected to have many openings is registered nurses. The median age of registered nurses is increasing, and not enough younger workers are replacing them. As a result, employers in some parts of the country are reporting difficulties in attracting and retaining nurses.

Hottest Jobs. Employment in this field is projected to grow by 25.1 percent from 2008 to 2018. All of the following occupations employed more than 100,000 workers in 2008 and are projected to grow within this industry by at least 35.3 percent. Note that the following facts about these occupations apply only to workers *within this industry*. For more generalized information about these occupations, see Part II.

Hottest Jobs in Health Care

Occupation	Occupational Growth Within Industry	Workforce Size Within Industry	Average Earnings Within Industry
1. Physician Assistants	44.8%	230,320	$84,473
2. Physical Therapist Aides	43.7%	165,540	$23,941
3. Speech-Language Pathologists	41.4%	149,830	$72,509
4. Physical Therapist Assistants	41.1%	213,060	$48,367
5. Physical Therapists	40.6%	535,050	$74,846
6. Occupational Therapists	37.1%	229,690	$71,877
7. Dental Assistants	36.8%	1,127,240	$33,150

Occupation	Occupational Growth Within Industry	Workforce Size Within Industry	Average Earnings Within Industry
8. Dental Hygienists	36.7%	677,450	$67,536
9. Optometrists	35.4%	106,170	$96,500
10. Medical Assistants	35.3%	1,730,370	$28,779

Employment Services

What the Field Does. The employment services industry provides a variety of human resources services to businesses. These services include providing temporary workers to other businesses, helping employers locate suitable employees, and providing human resources services to clients.

The employment services industry has four distinct segments. *Employment placement agencies* list employment vacancies and place permanent employees. *Temporary help services,* also referred to as temporary staffing agencies, provide employees, on a contract basis and for a limited time, to clients in need of workers to supplement their labor force. *Executive search services,* often referred to as *headhunters,* provide search, recruitment, and placement services for clients with specific executive and senior management needs. *Professional employer organizations* are engaged in providing human resources and human resources management services to staff the businesses of clients.

Employment. Workers employed as permanent staff of employment agencies, temporary help services firms, or professional employer organizations usually work in offices and may meet numerous people daily. The temporary employees who are contracted out to clients typically work in a variety of environments and often do not stay in any one place long enough to settle into a personal workspace or establish close relationships with co-workers. Most assignments are of short duration because temporary workers may be called to replace a worker who is ill or on vacation or to help with a short-term surge of work. However, assignments of several weeks or longer occasionally may be offered.

Because temporary and leased workers are used by a variety of different businesses, the work environments can vary greatly, depending on the type of work done. Permanent employees who are responsible for the day-to-day activities of firms within the industry tend to work in offices.

Getting Started. The employment services industry offers opportunities in many occupations for workers with a variety of skill levels and experience. The majority of temporary jobs still require only graduation from high school or the equivalent, while some permanent jobs, such as those in management, may require a bachelor's or higher degree.

Some temporary help services firms offer skills training to newly hired employees to make them more marketable. The training may or may not be free.

Advancement as a temporary employee usually takes the form of pay increases or greater choice of jobs. More often, temporary workers transfer to full-time jobs with other employers.

Staff of employment placement agencies and permanent staff of temporary help services firms typically are made up of employment interviewers, administrative support workers, and managers. The qualifications required of employment interviewers depend partly on the occupations that the employment placement agency or temporary help services firm specializes in placing. For example, agencies that place professionals, such as accountants or nurses, usually employ interviewers with college degrees in similar fields.

Job Prospects. Increasing demand among employers for flexible work arrangements and schedules, coupled with significant turnover in these positions, should create plentiful job opportunities for persons who seek jobs as temporary or contract workers through 2018. In particular, suppliers of medical personnel to hospitals and other medical facilities should continue to perform well as demand for temporary health-care staffing grows to meet the needs of aging baby boomers and to supplement demand for more health-care services throughout the country.

Most new jobs will arise in the largest occupational groups in this industry—office and administrative support, production, and transportation and material-moving occupations. However, the continuing trend toward specialization also will spur growth among professional workers, including engineers and health-care practitioners such as registered nurses. Managers also will see an increase in new jobs as government increasingly contracts out management functions. In addition, growth of temporary help firms and professional employer organizations—which provide human resource management, risk management, accounting, and information technology services—will provide more opportunities for professional workers within those fields.

Hottest Jobs. Employment in this field is projected to grow by 18.7 percent from 2008 to 2018. All of the following occupations are projected to grow within this industry by at least 23.6 percent. Note that the following facts about these occupations apply only to workers *within this industry*. For more generalized information about these occupations, see Part II.

Hottest Jobs in Employment Services

Occupation	Occupational Growth Within Industry	Workforce Size Within Industry	Average Earnings Within Industry
1. Accountants and Auditors	38.9%	16,670	$55,870
2. Customer Service Representatives	35.9%	95,070	$27,690
3. Construction Laborers	33.8%	99,740	$23,200
4. Computer Software Engineers, Systems Software	33.8%	6,900	$92,480
5. Computer Software Engineers, Applications	33.7%	6,530	$92,010
6. Employment, Recruitment, and Placement Specialists	31.8%	77,070	$43,010
7. Maintenance and Repair Workers, General	28.0%	23,890	$30,920
8. Retail Salespersons	26.8%	16,240	$21,120
9. Home Health Aides	24.4%	19,890	$21,980
10. Production, Planning, and Expediting Clerks	23.6%	5,540	$34,820

Construction

What the Field Does. Houses, apartments, factories, offices, schools, roads, and bridges are only some of the products of the construction industry. Among this industry's activities are the building of new structures, including site preparation, plus additions and modifications to existing structures. The industry also includes maintenance, repair, and improvements on these structures.

The construction industry is divided into three major segments. The *construction of buildings* segment includes contractors, usually called general contractors, who build residential, industrial, commercial, and other buildings. *Heavy and civil engineering* construction contractors build sewers, roads, highways, bridges, tunnels, and other projects related to our nation's infrastructure. *Specialty trade* contractors perform specialized construction-related activities such as carpentry, painting, plumbing, and electrical work.

Construction usually is done or coordinated by general contractors, who specialize in one type of construction such as residential or commercial building. They take full responsibility for the complete job, except for specified portions of the work that may be omitted from the general contract. Although general contractors may do a portion of the work with their own crews, they often subcontract most of the work to heavy construction or specialty trade contractors.

Employment. Most employees in the construction industry work full time, and many work over 40 hours a week. In 2008, about 18 percent of construction workers worked 45 hours or more a week. Construction workers may sometimes work evenings, weekends, and holidays to finish a job or take care of an emergency. Rain, snow, or wind may halt construction work. Workers in this industry usually do not get paid if they can't work due to inclement weather.

Workers in this industry need physical stamina because the work frequently requires prolonged standing, bending, stooping, and working in cramped quarters. They also may be required to lift and carry heavy objects. Exposure to the weather is common because much of the work is done outside or in partially enclosed structures. Construction workers often work with potentially dangerous tools and equipment amidst a clutter of building materials; some work on temporary scaffolding or at great heights. Consequently, they are more prone to injuries than workers in other jobs. To avoid injury, employees wear safety clothing, such as gloves; hard hats; and devices to protect their eyes, mouth, or hearing, as needed.

In 2008, about 64 percent of wage and salary jobs in construction were in the specialty trade contractors sector, primarily plumbing, heating, and air-conditioning; electrical; and masonry. Around 23 percent of jobs were in residential and nonresidential building construction. The rest were in heavy and civil engineering construction.

Most of the establishments in this field tend to be small; 68 percent employed fewer than 5 workers. About 12 percent of workers are employed by these very small contractors. Construction offers more opportunities than most other industries for individuals who want to own and run their own business.

Getting Started. Workers can enter the construction industry through a variety of educational and training backgrounds. Those entering construction out of high school usually start as laborers, helpers, or apprentices. While some laborers and helpers can learn their job in a few days, the skills required for many tradesworkers' jobs take years to learn and are usually learned through some combination of classroom instruction and on-the-job training.

Construction tradesworkers and mechanical and installation workers most often get their formal instruction by attending a local technical or trade school, participating in an apprenticeship, or taking part in an employer-provided training program. In addition, they learn their craft by working with more experienced workers. Most construction tradesworkers' jobs require proficiency in reading and mathematics. Safety training is also required for most jobs; English language skills are essential for workers to advance within their trade.

A few occupations (for example, electricians and plumbers) have licensing requirements. There are often separate licenses for contractors and workers. Licenses and certifications need to be renewed on a regular basis.

Managerial personnel usually have a college degree or considerable experience in their specialty. Individuals who enter construction with college degrees usually start as management trainees or as assistants to construction managers. Those who receive degrees in construction science often start as field engineers, schedulers, or cost estimators.

Job Prospects. The construction industry was strongly affected by the credit crisis and recession that began in December 2007. Housing prices fell and foreclosures of homes rose sharply, particularly in overbuilt areas of the country. New housing construction, while still ongoing, dropped significantly. However, the recovery is expected to release pent-up demand for construction work. "Green construction" is an area that is increasingly popular and involves making buildings as environmentally friendly and energy efficient as possible by using more recyclable and earth-friendly products.

Job opportunities are expected to be good, especially for experienced and skilled construction tradesworkers, because of the need to replace the large number of workers anticipated to leave these occupations over the next decade.

Certain occupations should have particularly good job opportunities. Because of the difficulty in obtaining certification as a crane operator, some employers have been unable to fill some positions. Electricians, plumbers, pipefitters, and steamfitters are also licensed occupations that should have a favorable outlook due to projected job growth. Roofers should have favorable opportunities due to job growth and difficult working conditions, which lead to high replacement needs. Boilermakers; brickmasons, block-masons, and stonemasons; and structural and reinforcing iron and rebar workers should have excellent opportunities because of the skills required to perform their duties and the difficult working conditions. Installation and maintenance occupations—including line installers and heating and air-conditioning mechanics and installers—also should have especially favorable prospects because of a growing stock of homes that will require service to maintain interior systems. Construction managers who have a bachelor's degree in construction science with an emphasis on construc-tion management and related work experience in construction management services firms should have especially good prospects as well. Employment growth among administrative support occupations will continue to be limited by office automation. Construction laborers needing less training should face competition for work because there are few barriers to entrance to this occupation.

The number of job openings in construction may fluctuate from year to year. New construction is usually cut back during periods when the econo-my is not expanding or interest rates are high.

Hottest Jobs. Employment in this field is projected to grow by 18.7 per-cent from 2008 to 2018. All of the following occupations are projected to grow within this industry by at least 30.6 percent. Note that the following facts about these occupations apply only to workers *within this industry.* For more generalized information about these occupations, see Part II.

Hottest Jobs in Construction

Occupation	Occupational Growth Within Industry	Workforce Size Within Industry	Average Earnings Within Industry
1. Heating, Air Conditioning, and Refrigeration Mechanics and Installers	43.0%	710,030	$39,320
2. Septic Tank Servicers and Sewer Pipe Cleaners	37.8%	14,250	$34,130
3. Telecommunications Equipment Installers and Repairers, Except Line Installers	35.3%	89,950	$40,640
4. Purchasing Agents, Except Wholesale, Retail, and Farm Products	33.6%	53,230	$50,410

Occupation	Occupational Growth Within Industry	Workforce Size Within Industry	Average Earnings Within Industry
5. Cost Estimators	33.1%	439,400	$59,500
6. Security and Fire Alarm Systems Installers	33.0%	82,390	$38,600
7. Industrial Machinery Mechanics	31.3%	12,410	$40,340
8. Mechanical Engineers	31.2%	10,090	$73,730
9. Electrical and Electronics Repairers, Commercial and Industrial Equipment	30.9%	29,010	$47,040
10. Customer Service Representatives	30.6%	52,480	$32,750

Child Day Care Services

What the Field Does. Obtaining affordable, quality child day care, especially for children under age 5, is a major concern for many parents, particularly in recent years with the rise in families with two working parents. As the need for child day care increases, the child day care services industry continues to expand.

Two main types of child care make up this industry: center-based care and family child care. Formal child day care centers include part- and full-day preschools, child care centers, school- and community-based prekindergartens, and Head Start and Early Head Start centers. Family child care providers care for children in their home for a fee and are the majority of self-employed workers in this industry.

The for-profit part of this industry includes centers that operate independently or as part of a local or national company. The number of for-profit establishments has grown rapidly in response to demand for child care services. Within the nonprofit sector, there has been strong growth in Head Start and Early Head Start, the federally funded child care programs designed to provide disadvantaged children with social, educational, and health services.

Some employers offer child care benefits to their employees, recognizing that the unavailability of child care is a barrier to the employment of many parents, especially women, and that the cost of the benefits is offset by increased employee morale and productivity and reduced absenteeism.

Employment. Many child day care centers are open 12 or more hours a day and cannot close until all the children are picked up by their parents or guardians. Unscheduled overtime, traffic jams, and other types of emergencies can cause parents or guardians to be late. The industry also offers many opportunities for part-time work: More than 29 percent of all employees worked part time in 2008.

Helping children grow, learn, and gain new skills can be very rewarding, but the work can be physically taxing, as workers constantly stand, walk, bend, stoop, and lift to attend to each child's needs, interests, and problems.

Jobs in child day care are found across the country, mirroring the distribution of the population. However, day care centers are less common in rural areas, where there are fewer children to support a separate facility. Child day care operations vary in size, from the self-employed person caring for a few children in a private home to the large corporate-sponsored center employing a sizable staff. Almost 86 percent of all wage and salary jobs in 2008 were located in establishments with fewer than 50 employees.

Opportunities for self-employment in this industry are among the best in the economy, partly because it is easy to start a business in this field.

Getting Started. Most states do not regulate family child care providers who care for just a few children, typically between ages 2 and 5. Providers who care for more children are required to be licensed and, in a few states, must have some minimal training. Once a provider joins the industry, most states require the worker to complete a number of hours of training per year. In nearly all states, licensing regulations require criminal record checks for all child day care staff.

For workers at child care centers, most states have established minimum educational or training requirements. Training requirements are most stringent for directors, less so for teachers, and minimal for child care workers and teacher assistants. In many centers, directors must have a college degree, often with experience in child day care and specific training in early childhood development. Teachers must have a high school diploma and, in many cases, a combination of college education and experience. Assistants and child care workers usually need a high school diploma, but that is not always a requirement. Many states also mandate other types of training for staff members, such as on health and first aid, fire safety, and child abuse detection and prevention.

Job Prospects. Opportunities within this industry are expected to be excellent because of the need to replace workers who choose to leave the industry to return to school or enter a new occupation or industry. Replacement needs are substantial, reflecting the low wages and relatively meager benefits provided to most workers.

Hottest Jobs. Employment in this field is projected to grow by 15.5 percent from 2008 to 2018. The following list of high-growth jobs in the industry is shorter than the lists for most other industries. This is partly because many of the jobs in this industry are low-paying, and all job lists in this book exclude low-paying jobs. In addition, jobs in this industry are concentrated in a smaller number of occupations than in most other industries. All of the occupations on the list are projected to grow within this industry by at least 11.9 percent. Note that the following facts about these occupations apply only to workers *within this industry*. For more generalized information about these occupations, see Part II.

Hottest Jobs in Child Day Care Services

Occupation	Occupational Growth Within Industry	Workforce Size Within Industry	Average Earnings Within Industry
1. Preschool Teachers, Except Special Education	22.8%	297,090	$22,700
2. Special Education Teachers, Preschool, Kindergarten, and Elementary School	22.8%	5,880	$34,400
3. Office Clerks, General	12.1%	9,200	$22,520
4. Kindergarten Teachers, Except Special Education	12.0%	8,140	$28,880
5. First-Line Supervisors/Managers of Personal Service Workers	12.0%	9,670	$29,150
6. Child, Family, and School Social Workers	12.0%	7,610	$31,170
7. Education Administrators, Preschool and Child Care Center/Program	11.9%	33,860	$37,740

Advocacy, Grantmaking, and Civic Organizations

What the Field Does. Advocacy, grantmaking, and civic organizations work to better their communities by directly addressing issues of public concern through service, independent action, or civic engagement. These organizations span the political spectrum of ideas and encompass every aspect of human endeavor, from symphonies to little leagues and from homeless shelters and day care centers to natural resource conservation advocates. These organizations often are collectively called "nonprofits," a name that is used to describe institutions and organizations that are neither government nor business.

Business, professional, labor, political, and similar organizations promote the business interests of their members. They include organizations such as chambers of commerce, real estate boards, and manufacturers' and trade associations.

Civic and social organizations promote the interests of communities who share common civic or social interests. These include alumni associations, automobile clubs, booster clubs, youth scouting organizations, parent-teacher associations, fraternal lodges, ethnic associations, and veterans' membership organizations.

Social advocacy organizations promote a particular cause or work for the realization of a specific social or political goal to benefit either a broad segment of the population or a specific constituency. This includes human rights organizations and environment, conservation, and wildlife organizations, among others.

Grantmaking and giving services include foundations and other organizations that mainly raise funds for social welfare activities, such as health, educational, scientific, and cultural activities.

Some organizations in this field receive most of their funds from private contributions, and the widespread use of the Internet has facilitated fund-raising and membership drives. Other organizations raise funds by charging fees for goods or services. Some have formed partnerships with for-profit corporations or government.

Employment. The work environment in this field generally is positive—workers know that their work helps people and improves their communities. However, fund-raising can be stressful, and workers employed in the direct delivery of social services may suffer from the same burnout experienced by many other workers in helping occupations.

Establishments in this field are found throughout the nation, but the greatest numbers of jobs are found in California and New York, the states with the greatest population. Most establishments in this industry are small; the majority of jobs are in establishments that employ fewer than 50 people.

Getting Started. The types of jobs and skills required in this field vary with the type and size of the organization. But all organizations need workers with strong communication and fund-raising skills, because they must constantly mobilize public support for their activities. Creativity and initiative are important, as many workers are responsible for a wide range of activities. Basic knowledge about accounting, finance, management, information systems, advertising, and marketing provide an important advantage for those trying to enter the field. In some cases, a second language may be needed for jobs that involve international activities. This highly competitive industry also needs individuals who have adequate technical skills to efficiently operate and maintain their computer systems.

Some workers prepare for a job by gaining experience as volunteers. Volunteering allows you to try out an organization to see whether you like it, to make good contacts in the industry, and to demonstrate a commitment to a cause. Many professionals in the industry begin their careers by getting experience in for-profit businesses.

Job Prospects. Civic and social organizations will experience increased demand as the population grows and as people continue to value the interests and connections they make as part of these groups. In particular, as the population ages and as more people enter retirement, demand for organizations that cater to these individuals will increase.

Professional occupations in this field are projected to grow faster than jobs in clerical and other support functions. In addition to employment growth, a large number of job openings should result from turnover as workers retire or leave the industry for other reasons, such as the industry's relatively low wages.

Hottest Jobs. Employment in this field is projected to grow by 14.1 percent from 2008 to 2018. All of the following occupations are projected to grow within this industry by at least 20.6 percent. Note that the following facts about these occupations apply only to workers *within this industry*. For more generalized information about these occupations, see Part II.

Hottest Jobs in Advocacy, Grantmaking, and Civic Organizations

Occupation	Occupational Growth Within Industry	Workforce Size Within Industry	Average Earnings Within Industry
1. Network Systems and Data Communications Analysts	52.9%	5,860	$64,782
2. Compliance Officers, Except Agriculture, Construction, Health and Safety, and Transportation	35.8%	5,300	$60,843
3. Compensation, Benefits, and Job Analysis Specialists	26.2%	10,010	$55,804
4. Market Research Analysts	26.0%	9,040	$52,531
5. Customer Service Representatives	25.8%	54,450	$28,135
6. Public Relations Specialists	25.1%	95,070	$51,256
7. Training and Development Specialists	25.0%	14,050	$55,445
8. Coaches and Scouts	24.2%	20,720	$23,164
9. Editors	21.2%	7,920	$56,930
10. Health Educators	20.6%	13,030	$40,257

Educational Services

What the Field Does. The educational services industry includes a variety of institutions that offer academic education, career and technical instruction, and other forms of education and training to millions of students each year.

At the K–12 level, education has become the subject of national concern because high school completion rates remain low, particularly for minority students, and employers contend that numerous high school graduates still lack many of the math and communication skills needed in today's workplace.

Employment. Most elementary and secondary schools generally operate 10 months a year, but administrators and many support staff often work the entire year. Postsecondary institutions operate year-round but may have reduced offerings during summer months. Institutions that cater to adult students, as well as those that offer educational support services such as tutoring, also may operate year-round. Night and weekend work is common for teachers of adult literacy and remedial and self-enrichment education, postsecondary teachers, and library workers in postsecondary institutions. Part-time work is common for this same group of teachers, as well as for teacher assistants and school bus drivers. Many teachers spend significant time outside of school preparing for class, doing administrative tasks, conducting research, writing articles and books, and pursuing advanced degrees.

The educational services industry was the second-largest industry in the economy in 2008, providing jobs for about 13.5 million wage and salary workers. Although 67 percent of these workers are employed in professional and related occupations, the industry also employs many administrative support, managerial, service, and other workers.

Getting Started. The educational services industry employs some of the most highly educated workers in the labor force. About 64 percent of employees have at least a bachelor's degree, because a bachelor's degree is required for nearly all professional occupations in the industry. Many professional occupations also require a master's degree or doctorate, particularly for jobs at postsecondary institutions or in administration.

The training and qualifications required of preschool teachers vary widely. Each state has its own licensing requirements, ranging from a high school diploma to a college degree.

K–12 teachers in public schools must have a bachelor's degree and complete an approved teacher training program, with a prescribed number of subject and education credits, as well as supervised practice teaching. All states require public school teachers to be licensed; however, licensure requirements vary by state. Many states offer alternative licensure programs for people who have bachelor's degrees in the subject they will teach but lack the education courses required for a regular license.

Most other professionals in public schools, such as guidance counselors, librarians, and administrators, need master's degrees.

Training requirements for teacher assistants range from a high school diploma to an associate degree.

Postsecondary teachers who teach at four-year colleges and universities generally must have a doctoral or other terminal degree for full-time, tenure-track employment, and usually also for part-time teaching at these institutions as well, though a master's degree is sometimes sufficient. At two-year colleges, however, most positions are held by teachers with master's degrees.

Job Prospects. School districts, particularly those in urban and rural areas, continue to report difficulties in recruiting qualified teachers, administrators, and support personnel. Fast-growing areas of the country—including several states and cities in the South and West—also report difficulty recruiting education workers, especially teachers. Currently, alternative licensing programs are helping to attract more people into teaching, especially those from other career paths, but opportunities should continue to be very good for highly qualified teachers, especially those in subject areas with the highest needs, such as math, science, and special education.

At the postsecondary level, increases in student enrollments and projected retirements of current faculty should contribute to a favorable job market for postsecondary teachers. However, candidates applying for tenured positions will continue to face keen competition as many colleges and universities rely on adjunct or part-time faculty and graduate students to make up a larger share of the total instructional staff than in the past.

Hottest Jobs. Employment in this field is projected to grow by 12.5 percent from 2008 to 2018. All of the following occupations are projected to grow within this industry by at least 27.6 percent. (It's especially striking to note that very few of these jobs are for traditional classroom teachers.) Note that the following facts about these occupations apply only to workers *within this industry*. For more generalized information about these occupations, see Part II.

Hottest Jobs in Educational Services

Occupation	Occupational Growth Within Industry	Workforce Size Within Industry	Average Earnings Within Industry
1. Network Systems and Data Communications Analysts	51.7%	12,740	$60,270
2. Self-Enrichment Education Teachers	49.6%	106,580	$37,950
3. Customer Service Representatives	44.7%	16,630	$30,120
4. Loan Counselors	39.4%	12,900	$37,360
5. Medical Scientists, Except Epidemiologists	34.6%	29,580	$56,790
6. Employment, Recruitment, and Placement Specialists	33.9%	10,590	$46,040
7. Training and Development Specialists	33.3%	16,430	$51,790
8. Police and Sheriff's Patrol Officers	30.3%	17,020	$44,980

Occupation	Occupational Growth Within Industry	Workforce Size Within Industry	Average Earnings Within Industry
9. Coaches and Scouts	29.4%	131,810	$28,100
10. Instructional Coordinators	27.6%	93,820	$60,510

Where to Find Out More About Fields

For in-depth profiles of the 11 hot fields covered by this chapter, plus 32 other fields, browse through the Department of Labor's *Career Guide to Industries*, a Web-only publication, at www.bls.gov/oco/cg/.

From Fields to Jobs

You know I'm not going to let you finish this chapter without taking some kind of *action*. Your task now, if you haven't done it already, is to circle several intriguing jobs in this chapter's hottest-jobs lists. Then read about them in Part II. And, finally, explore the ones that still appeal to you, using some of the resources listed in the last section of the appendix.

Key Points: Chapter 3

- Some fields are growing more rapidly than others and will provide lots of job opportunities.

- You also can find jobs in slow-growing fields.

- Within each field, some jobs are especially promising over the coming decade.

CHAPTER 4

Bridge to Your Goal

I n this chapter, you're going to consider the *gap* you're facing now and how you're going to bridge it.

What gap? You're reading this chapter because your 2011 career goal is to move to a new employer, a new industry, or a new occupation. Odds are you're not completely ready to make that move.

So you're looking at a space between where you are now and where you want to get to. Maybe the gap is just a slit. Maybe it's a chasm. But that's the gap you're going to address here.

This chapter covers four likely gaps and, for each one, suggests two or more possible action plans to *bridge* the gap. Find the gap that best describes your situation, and you'll see various ways you can bridge it. Finally, at the end of the chapter, be sure to commit to some specific actions you can take to build your bridges.

Gap: You Don't Have the Skills You Need

You have investigated a new employer, a new industry, or a new occupation, and you realize that you are not yet qualified to make this move: You don't have the skills that are expected.

Bridge: Skills Training

Even beyond your 2011 career move, you'll need to work on your skills just to stay in the same job. Fortunately, businesses and educational institutions are aware of the need for lifelong learning, so opportunities for acquiring new skills are better now than they have ever been—if you are willing to take the initiative to seek them out.

Informal On-the-Job Learning

If you're already working, even part-time, you can develop new skills on the job. When you see co-workers using skills that you don't have, ask them to show you how. When you feel you have mastered the skill, ask your supervisor for an assignment that uses the skill—perhaps not a high-stakes project, but something that will demonstrate your new skill. Then ask for feedback that specifically targets your use of the skill. Try not to be defensive in response to criticism; use this feedback as part of the learning process.

Informal Learning Through Volunteer Work

If you're not working now, you can get informal training in specific skills by doing volunteer work in a relevant setting. For example, to improve your people skills, do volunteer work at a senior center or a charity fund-raising event. Some hobbies also provide opportunities for you to learn skills—for example, designing Web pages, customizing cars, or gardening. With hobbies, it helps to join a club so you can learn from more highly skilled hobbyists and get feedback on your accomplishments. Just keep in mind that your volunteer work can do more than just help others and your hobby can be more than just a self-indulgence. Use them as skill academies and then find ways to transfer those skills to your career.

Single Courses and Workshops

A course usually consists of multiple classes over a period of time; a workshop usually is a single session. Either can be useful for acquiring new skills. If the learning opportunity covers a highly job-relevant subject, it may be more practical for you to learn this way than to pursue another degree—particularly when you already have a degree. Night schools and corporate training centers offer courses in technical skills, such as using spreadsheets or driving trucks, or in "soft" skills, such as conducting meetings or reading people's body language. Another setting for training is the annual conference of the professional association relevant to your career, where you can attend training workshops.

Self-Instruction

Sometimes you can create your own training program by studying a book or technical manual. Consider the time and expense of self-training as investments in your future employability. Try to find one or two study partners to learn with you; study partners help reinforce each other's learning. (With more than three members, study groups usually are less effective.) Because you bring different perspectives, sometimes your partner can solve a problem or explain a concept that stumps you. To measure progress, quiz each other. Finally, your study partner is a witness who can confirm that you have mastered the material.

Gap: You Don't Have a Formal Credential That You Need

Some skills can be learned only in formal settings. Secondary school teachers, for example, need a college degree and courses in education. Even in many jobs that do not have educational requirements spelled out by law, it will be necessary for you to work toward eventually obtaining a certain expected level of education.

Bridge: Formal Education or Training

This book does not have space for a full discussion of how to choose and apply to a college or other postsecondary school to get education or training. You can learn about those procedures elsewhere. However, I want you to think about the many options you have for getting formal credentials.

College Credit for What You Already Know

If you have learned a lot informally, you may be able to get college credit for your accomplishments. Keep in mind that all the methods described here involve fees, but they are cheaper than paying tuition and may fit into your schedule better than taking classes.

Several "colleges without walls" specialize in granting credit for experiential learning; you can get credit, even a degree, without visiting the college or residing in its state. But to prove you have learned at the college level, you need to assemble a portfolio of your work, something a lot more detailed than a statement on a resume.

Colleges Offering Credit for Portfolios

Thomas Edison State College: www.tesc.edu

Charter Oak State College: www.charteroak.edu

Excelsior College: www.excelsior.edu

Another way to prove your learning and get college credit is by taking a test. The College-Level Examination Program (CLEP) is the best-known program of this kind, and its credits are more widely accepted than those from any other such program. The tests are multiple choice and take 90 minutes. You can probably find study guides for specific CLEP tests at your local library. Other programs of this kind are DSST, which started in the military as the DANTES program; the Excelsior College Examinations; and the Thomas Edison College Examination Program (TECEP).

Credit by Examination

CLEP: www.collegeboard.com/clep

DSST: www.getcollegecredit.com

Excelsior College Examinations: www.excelsior.edu

TECEP: http://www.tesc.edu/701.php

Beware of scams. Because there is such a demand for education and the costs of education have risen rapidly, a lot of "diploma mills" are offering bogus degrees without requiring classes or any in-depth demonstration of college-level work. As in all cases of fraud, if it sounds too good to be true, it probably is. Before you sign up with an education provider, make sure the institution is recognized by the Council on Higher Education Accreditation (CHEA) or the U.S. Department of Education. Don't accept another accrediting organization. And you should never consider using a phony degree to pad your resume. It's against the law in a growing number of states, and law enforcement officials are investigating diploma mills and publicizing their names so employers will be on the lookout.

College Credit for Military Training

If you have acquired college-level skills in military training, you may want to use one of the examination programs discussed in the previous section. But you may be able to obtain college credit more directly. Many colleges follow the recommendations of the American Council on Education (ACE) in awarding college credit for specific military experiences. Even some *employers* use the *ACE Guide* to recognize military experiences that are equivalent to academic coursework. You may be able to convince an employer that your military service gives you the credentials needed for the job. The *ACE Guide* is online at www.militaryguides.acenet.edu.

Apprenticeship as a Training Route

Apprenticeship is a system of job training in which trainees become highly skilled workers through a combination of worksite and classroom learning. It is sometimes called "the other four-year degree" because it often takes four years and it results in a nationally recognized credential that can open the door to income and job security that may be as good as or better than what college graduates enjoy.

Apprenticeship has been used as a form of training for thousands of years, and worksite learning has always been at its core. Apprentices are supervised and taught by experienced workers who can pass on skills, work habits, strategies for problem solving, and field-specific lore that often cannot be learned anywhere else. To learn all this, apprentices need to do more than just watch experienced workers or act as "helpers." They perform real work tasks at higher and higher levels of skill, and they are rotated through all aspects of the job so that they learn the full range of skills.

Because modern jobs involve technology and take place in a complex business world, apprenticeships usually include a component of classroom learning. These classes typically meet after working hours and may be held at a community college or a vocational school, by correspondence, or even on the Web.

Most forms of learning cost money, and college tuition is getting more expensive at an alarming rate. But apprentices earn while they learn. They start out at a rate of pay that is often only half the hourly rate of a fully qualified worker, but as they gain work experience they get regular increases in pay. Of course, these increases depend on satisfactory performance at the worksite and in classes. During the last phase of the apprenticeship, they typically earn 90 percent of a fully qualified worker's hourly rate. Apprentices may also receive health insurance or retirement benefits.

The Military Training Route

The military can be a lifetime career, but most recruits serve only a few years in uniform. They get training in specific job skills and in military work-related attitudes and then leave active duty to pursue a civilian career.

The military covers a range of jobs almost as diverse as those found in the civilian workplace, which means that the skills you learn in the military may qualify you for employment in a good job after you hang up your uniform—for example, as a dental hygienist, a fire fighter, a dispensing optician, a plumber, or a truck driver, to name a few.

Your commitment to the military is for eight years. Your contract may specify only a portion of that time as active duty—as little as two years in some jobs and service branches. Theoretically, after this period of active duty you could ride out the remainder of your eight-year commitment in the Individual Ready Reserves, wearing a uniform only for annual inspections. However, if the military needs you, they have the right to keep you on active duty or in the drilling reserves or, having released you, to recall you to one of those roles at any time during your eight-year commitment.

Normally you will be free to hold a civilian job during any periods of inactivity within your eight-year commitment, but of course that career may be interrupted if you are called up again. Federal law prohibits your employer from discriminating against you because of your military obligations. In reality, however, a military call-up can be either a trivial or a serious interference with your career, depending on what type of job you hold. For example, if you are self-employed as a civilian, a military call-up can mean a significant cut in your income.

When you enlist, you give up many freedoms of civilian life, but many of the basic requirements of life are provided for you while you are on active duty. You get a place to live, all your meals, complete health care, recreation, worship services—and a salary that, although it is not outstanding, is not low when received on top of all these other benefits. Most important, you not only get a job, but all the training you need for the job, and you are encouraged to get additional training to build your skills.

Although the military does a lot of training, its core business is defense, and that sometimes can require combat. Even training exercises can be dangerous. The risks to life and limb are real. Still, very few jobs come with the satisfaction of having put your life on the line for the safety and freedom of your fellow citizens.

The Two-Year College Route

A bachelor's degree does open doors. But many people find happiness in jobs that require only an associate degree obtained through two years of college. These people enter the workforce without spending many years in college. They don't pile up debt to pay for many years of tuition. They don't study many theoretical subjects that are not relevant to the job. Instead, they learn the work tasks and skills in a full-time, two-year program that is _custom-made to prepare for the job_ and that leads to an associate degree.

Associate degrees are offered by community colleges, junior colleges, technical colleges, and some colleges that also offer four-year degrees. Traditionally, you need to complete high school before entering an associate degree program, but the entrance requirements are usually easier to meet than they would be for a four-year program. Some high schools and community colleges work together to give students still in high school credit toward their associate degrees.

Most two-year programs focus on a particular career goal. If the goal is a career that requires you to pass a certification or licensing test, make sure the program covers all the subjects needed for the test.

If you think you may want to pursue a bachelor's degree sometime in the future, be sure that your associate degree program will be accepted as the equivalent of two years' coursework toward a bachelor's degree in a related field. Some programs, especially at technical colleges, focus so much on hands-on learning that they leave little time for the theoretical subjects (such as mathematics and English) that you need to continue learning in the future.

The Four-Year College Route

A bachelor's degree can provide you with many advantages in the job market. In fact, some jobs require it. For example, to become licensed as a professional engineer or a public school teacher, you generally need to have a bachelor's degree from an approved program. In many other occupations there is no legal requirement, but employers will not consider job candidates who do not have at least a bachelor's degree, sometimes in a specific major.

In addition to giving you a broad and deep knowledge of a field, a bachelor's degree gives you a foundation for further learning by teaching you skills that go beyond the immediate demands of a job—skills in critical thinking, writing, math, and research methods. The degree represents a commitment of time and energy that employers respect. Employers also believe that bachelor's-degree holders have a broad understanding of the society in which business is conducted and the flexibility to adapt as the career undergoes change.

On average, the degree leads to better-paying and more secure jobs. The BLS reports that, in 2008, people who held a bachelor's degree earned an average of $1,012 per week and had an unemployment rate of 2.8 percent. That compares to $618 per week and 5.7 percent for those who had only a high school diploma.

Finally, the degree enriches your life beyond your job. It gives you a context in which to get more out of experiences such as a nature walk, a conversation with a person much older than you, a movie, a visit to a foreign country, a political speech, or a news article about an emerging technology.

Which Route Is Best for You?

Only you can decide which route for formal credentials is your best bet. For some routes, you can use a toe-in-the-water approach; for example, you might take one or two college courses to decide whether you have the interest and ability to make the commitment to a two- or four-year degree. For other routes, especially the military, you can't "test drive" the experience beforehand.

The best way to evaluate an educational or training program (including self-instruction) is to get several opinions about it. Don't let a slick sales pitch be your only indication of what lies ahead. Talk to workers who have learned their job skills through this route. Talk to employers about what background they prefer for the workers they hire.

Gap: You're Not Yet Ready to "Sell" Yourself

Let's assume that by now you've figured out *which* occupation, industry, or kind of employer is your 2011 career goal. But can you tell me, while standing on one foot, *why* you're the person who should get this kind of job? Why you instead of somebody else?

Bridge: Identifying and Documenting Your Brand

You need to be able to tell employers clearly and concisely *what you can bring to the table*, both in spoken and written form.

Identifying Your Brand

Employers want to know what you have to offer and what qualifies you to hold the specific job in the context of their business. Some people have difficulty talking about their skills and experience out of fear of appearing boastful. Colin Frager, an executive recruiter and CEO of the Colin Phillips Group, says it helps to think of yourself not as a person, but as a product or service that you're selling to the employer. This allows you to be objective about your strengths and also helps guide your research into employers' needs.

Ideally, you'll be able to think of yourself as a brand. Just as it's easy to summarize Volvo as the really safe car or Apple as the computer manufacturer with the really cool devices, you should be able to think of yourself as having some special attribute or record of achievement that defines what you have to offer an employer. Okay, what's *your* brand? What's going to make the employer want to hire you instead of dozens of other people with impressive resumes?

This process of focusing on your brand can take hours or even months, but it is much more productive than sending off nontargeted resumes like a dandelion puff scattering its seeds. You wouldn't think of entering an athletic competition without months or years of preparation. What makes you think you can compete in the job market without preparing first?

Creating Your Elevator Speech

Once you have clarified your focus, you should prepare and rehearse an elevator speech. This is a brief statement of who you are, what kind of job you're seeking, and why you qualify for this kind of job. No matter where you use this speech, it must be concise enough that you could say it to someone on an elevator and get all your points across before the elevator has stopped. You can practice using this speech, or at least parts of it, whenever anyone asks you what you do for a living (which is a very common question). Instead of giving merely a job title and letting the other person assume that you fit various stereotypes about that occupation, say things about your background and aspirations.

Focusing Your Resume

Your resume needs to focus on your brand, starting with what the resume says about your career goal. Remember, "I'll find *something*" is not a career plan for 2011. Your resume (and also any cover letters) should focus on a particular objective.

A multi-page resume that reflects a lot of work experience can blur your focus and probably needs a one-page executive summary so readers can quickly identify what you seek and what you have to offer. Conversely, the resume may benefit from an additional detailed document, headed something like "Key Initiatives and Successes," that highlights your record of achievement for those readers who want more specifics. (Some even include graphs.)

This book does not have room for examples of these documents, but here are some JIST books about resume writing that should prove helpful:

- *Résumé Magic: Trade Secrets of a Professional Résumé Writer,* by Susan Britton Whitcomb
- *The Career Coward's Guide to Resumes,* by Katy Piotrowski, MEd
- *Amazing Resumes,* by Jim Bright, PhD, and Joanne Earl, PhD
- *30-Minute Resume Makeover,* by Louise Kursmark

Gap: You Don't Know About Any Job Openings

Eventually, the career plans covered by this chapter all come down to the same thing: finding a job. In 2011, the odds of rapid success are much better than they were a couple of years before, but it's rarely an easy task. What's the best way?

Bridge: Finding the Hidden Job Market

You may have already heard about the "hidden job market." Studies have revealed that most jobs are found not by answering an advertisement in a newspaper or by waiting for a Web site to match you to an employer, but rather through two basic strategies: **cold-calling** employers who hire people like you or **networking** so that you hear about potential job openings. The two overlap to some extent: Through a cold call to an employer, you may hear about a possible job elsewhere, and through your network, you may hear about employers who are most likely to be worth cold-calling. You can pursue both strategies simultaneously.

Both networking and cold-calling require you to move outside your comfort zone. Your problem is that you don't know about these hidden job openings. You won't learn about them by talking only to your friends, because your friends tend to know only the same things you know. The principle behind networking is that by connecting to *the people your friends know* you can learn information (in this case, about jobs) that ordinarily would not be available to you. The principle behind cold-calling is that by talking directly to *the people who make hiring decisions*, you can learn about jobs that may never be advertised.

Don't undertake either of these steps without first clarifying and documenting your brand, as discussed previously.

Networking

You *already* have a network. Now, it's a matter of using it. Your network includes more than your close friends and relatives. It includes anyone who knows about you and how to get in touch with you.

All these people have connections to people you don't know, people who may know about jobs. Give them your elevator speech and make it clear to them what sort of work you're looking for. You may also find it useful to ask them for advice and look at this as a final stage of career exploration. For example, you might ask them what industries or businesses need people like you, or you might ask whether they know anyone who does this kind of work and what that person's experiences have been. Conversations like this plant a seed: These people now think of you as a job-seeker in this field and may later relay to you news of a job opening. More likely, they will be able to tell you the name of someone who is more knowledgeable about the field, and *that* person may be your actual lead for a job opening. Make a point of asking for the name of someone who knows lots of people in the field you're targeting. Studies of networks show that most contacts are made through a small number of very well-connected people.

A good way to expand your network is to join a professional association, go to meetings, and make contact with people in your field.

Cold-Calling

Someone in your network may mention your name to a manager who is hiring, and that person may give you a call. But, in many situations, the person in your network will give you the name of someone who is hiring, and it will be up to *you* to make the call. In that case, you are shifting to the cold-calling strategy.

When you make a cold call to a likely business, *don't* contact the human resources department; they know only about the part of the job market that isn't hidden. Instead, find the name and phone number of someone who has the power to make a hiring decision. In a small company, this may be the CEO or other top manager; in a large company, it may be a department head. Telephone this person. If you call between 8 and 9 in the morning or 5 and 6 in the evening, you may improve the odds that the phone will be answered by the person you seek rather than by a secretary. If you get the person's voice mailbox, hang up and try again at another time; cold calls are unlikely to be returned. E-mail takes less courage than the telephone, but it is too easily lost in the pile of messages cluttering your target's inbox and may automatically be flagged as spam. Still another way to make contact is to drop in on the business in person. This tends to work best at small businesses, where you can ask to speak to the person in charge; at a large organization, you are likely to be sent to the human resources department, where your job application and resume will be tucked into a file drawer and probably never be read again. Usually the best time to visit is early in the morning, before the person you want to speak to gets caught up in work tasks.

Once you are talking to a person who can make a hiring decision, you have two tactics open to you: direct and indirect. The direct method is to give your elevator speech, make it clear that you are interested in a job, and ask for an interview. Be prepared to ask several times, because this shows your interest and determination. Don't ask whether the business has job openings, but perhaps ask if the business is likely to have openings in the future. If the person on the other end says that the company is not hiring now, ask for a get-acquainted interview—maybe a lunch date. At the very least, ask for leads to people who might be hiring elsewhere, call those leads, and tell them who referred you. Expect a lot of rejection, but keep in mind that these calls take only a few minutes, so you can cover a large number of employers in one afternoon.

The indirect method is similar—it uses an elevator speech about your background and aims for an interview—but it stops short of asking for a _job_ interview. Instead, you treat the person like a highly targeted networking contact; the goal is an interview that will focus on _learning more information_ rather than on being hired. For example, you might say that you are thinking of specializing in the kind of work that goes on in that person's business and you want to learn more about the pros and cons of that specialization. If the person on the other end tries to cut you off by saying that the company is not hiring, make it clear that you are not asking for a job interview–you want information or perhaps advice. The informational interview may not, in fact, lead to a job at that company—at least not at present—but it may lead to a future job offer, and at least it has a good chance of taking your networking campaign to a higher level. This person is much more likely than your second cousin or your high school friend to know someone in another department or a similar business who has a job opening.

Commit to Some Bridge-Building Actions

Like all the other chapters, this one ends by asking you to commit to some actions. For each gap you admitted to in this chapter, in the list that follows, *circle at least one action* that will help build the appropriate bridge. Then turn to chapter 5 and learn the first steps you can take toward accomplishing the actions you've circled.

Gap: You Don't Have the Skills You Need
Bridge: Skills Training

Bridge-Building Action

Getting informal on-the-job training

Volunteering to get informal training

Taking a single class or workshop

Finding a study partner for self-instruction

Gap: You Don't Have a Formal Credential That You Need
Bridge: Formal Education or Training

Bridge-Building Action

Getting college credit for informal learning

Getting college credit for military training

Applying for a relevant apprenticeship

Applying to a relevant two-year college program

Applying to a relevant four-year college program

Gap: You're Not Yet Ready to "Sell" Yourself
Bridge: Identifying and Documenting Your Brand

Bridge-Building Action

Identifying what makes you stand out

Creating your elevator speech

Focusing your resume on your goal and brand

Gap: You Don't Know About Any Job Openings
Bridge: Finding the Hidden Job Market

Bridge-Building Action
Informing your network
Expanding your network
Making cold calls

Key Points: Chapter 4

- You now face at least one gap between where you are now in your career and where you want to go.

- Usually there are several good ways you can bridge these gaps and accomplish your goals.

CHAPTER 5

First Steps

You ended the last chapter by committing yourself to at least one bridge-building activity. But it's easy to procrastinate when you're unsure how to take the very first steps toward building a bridge. That's why, in this chapter, I'm going to help you make more *specific* action plans for getting started on those bridges. You'll see what you can do *now* to set your plan in motion toward your 2011 career goal. I'm not going to let you drag your feet!

This chapter is ordered according to the same gaps and bridges you considered in chapter 4, so skip any gaps that are *not* problems for you and go right to the gaps that are. Find the bridge-building actions that you circled in chapter 4—the actions you think will help you bridge a gap. Read the first step for accomplishing that action and then write in the date you intend to take that first step.

Gap: You Don't Have the Skills You Need

Bridge: Skills Training

Action: Get Informal On-the-Job Training

First Step: E-mail That Requests a Skill-Testing Assignment

Here's an e-mail you can send to your boss, after filling in the blank. Go ahead and play around with the wording if you like, but try to cover all the major points. If you'd rather not use e-mail to get this message across, you may use the ideas as the basis for a conversation with your boss.

E-mail That Requests Skill-Testing Assignment

I have been working on improving my _____ skills and would really appreciate some feedback from you regarding these skills. I believe a good way for me to get this feedback is to tackle a work task that requires these skills at a level beyond what you've seen me do in the past. If I handle the task correctly and demonstrate the skill, please let me know I've done so. If I make any mistakes, I want to know about them, too. Please let me know not just what I've done wrong, but how I can do the task better. I promise I won't be defensive about your comments.

I'm not asking for extra pay for doing this, and doing it would not imply I've been promoted. I also assure you that I won't let this extra task interfere with my usual work assignments. If necessary, I'll work on this task outside of my regular work hours.

Please give some thought to what task would be appropriate—a challenge, but not so difficult that I'm guaranteed to fail. If you're not sure, I can suggest some possible tasks that you can choose from. I'll be happy to answer any other questions you have about this experiment.

Date I'm going to start this first step: _____

Action: Volunteer to Get Informal Training

First Step: Phone Script for an Offer to Volunteer

Here's a script for a phone call you can make to offer your services as a volunteer. Fill in the blanks for an appropriate volunteer activity and a related activity for which you already have experience. You probably want to use a lot of your own wording rather than repeating this on the phone word-for-word. But try to mention all of the important points included here.

Phone Script for an Offer to Volunteer

Hello. I understand that you need volunteers to do _____.
I'd be glad to do this for your organization. I should point out right away that I don't have much experience doing _____, but I'm really eager to learn how. I do have some experience doing a related task, _____, so I should be able to learn this new task if someone shows me how. Probably the best way to start is for you to team me up

(continued)

(continued)

> with an experienced volunteer. I promise I'll try very hard to get up to speed quickly.
>
> When would be a good time to get started?

Date I'm going to start this first step: _____

Action: Take a Single Course or Workshop

First Step: Get Detailed Information

Following are some facts you need to know about the course or workshop before signing up. (For the sake of simplicity, I'll refer to it simply as a course.) Investigate by studying the promotional materials for the course. If these leave some questions unanswered, telephone or e-mail the course provider. Use check marks to indicate which statements are true.

Facts to Know Before Signing Up for a Course or Workshop

___ The expected learning outcomes of the course are clear to me.

___ The learning outcomes match the skill needs of a current or potential employer.

___ The learning outcomes contribute to a skill I want to develop.

___ The learning outcomes do not repeat what I already know.

___ The course has no prerequisites I can't meet.

___ I have evidence that the course provider can teach me successfully. (Examples: reputation of provider; testimonial of a course completer; demonstrated skill of a course completer; recommendation by my employer.)

___ I will learn more or better than I could by teaching myself instead.

___ I will be able to show evidence of how the course has improved my skills. (Examples: certificate of completion; documentation of a completed project.)

___ The course is offered at a time convenient for me.

___ The course is offered at a place convenient for me.

___ I can afford the cost of the course (perhaps by getting my employer to pay).

Note that you don't have to check off *every* statement, but the more you agree with, the better. If several of the statements are not checked, maybe this course is not a good move for your career.

Date I'm going to start this first step: _____

Action: Find a Study Partner for Self-Instruction

First Step: Recruit a Suitable Study Partner

It is possible to study a subject by yourself, but learning with one or two study partners is usually much more effective.

Following are some statements about a potential study partner. Use check marks to indicate which statements are true.

Characteristics of a Good Study Partner

___ This person is interested in learning the same skill that I want to learn.

___ For the skill that I want to learn, this person is now at roughly the same level.

___ For the skill that I want to learn, this person has roughly the same aptitude for learning.

___ This person is as committed as I am to keeping the study program going and staying on task.

___ This person and I can agree on what book (or other learning resource) to use in our program of study.

___ This person and I can get along reasonably well.

___ This person's schedule and mine allow time to meet regularly for study sessions.

___ This person is able to find time to do the homework required between meetings.

Ideally, you know which statements you feel positive about. It's possible, however, that you're unsure about some statements. For example, you may not know how committed the study partner is until you have started studying together. If you feel neutral about some statements, you may choose to give the person the benefit of the doubt, start studying with this person, and eventually decide whether the arrangement is working out.

On the other hand, if you *already* feel negative about several statements, maybe you should consider finding someone else as a study partner.

Date I'm going to start this first step: _____

Gap: You Don't Have a Formal Credential That You Need

Bridge: Formal Education or Training

Action: Get College Credit for Informal Learning

First Step: Verify That Your Informal Learning Deserves College Credit

Chapter 4 lists some organizations that award college credit for informal learning. However, before you attempt to get college credit from one of these organizations, you need to know that you have accomplished the kind and level of learning that they recognize.

Following are some statements about your informal learning. Use a check mark to indicate which statements are true.

Characteristics of College-Level Informal Learning

___ I have more than just experience; I have learned concepts and skills.

___ What I learned goes beyond what a high school graduate would know or be able to do.

___ What I learned is a subject that is taught in college (although maybe not every college offers it).

___ What I learned is up to date with the current state of that field of knowledge.

___ What I learned is transferable in some way; it does not apply to only one context.

___ I can demonstrate what I learned. (Examples: a performance; a portfolio of project outcomes; testimonial letters from supervisors; passing a college-level test.)

Note that you don't have to check off *every* statement, but the more you agree with, the better. If several of the statements are not checked, you may have difficulty persuading the organization to grant you credit. Remember to be wary of "diploma mill" scams.

Date I'm going to start this first step: _____

Action: Get College Credit for Military Training

First Step: Consult the Guide

You can find the *Guide to the Evaluation of Educational Experiences in the Armed Services* (also known as the *American Council on Education Guide*) online at www.militaryguides.acenet.edu. To find what college credit you may qualify for, you need to indicate either a **military occupation** you held or **a military training program** you completed. To narrow down your choices, it helps for you to specify your service branch.

You retrieve a list of matching occupations or training programs. Click on the one that reflects your actual experience, and you see a report that summarizes the skills you have learned and suggests an appropriate level and amount of college credit.

Although the *Guide* indicates you deserve a certain amount and type of college credit, not every college will actually grant that credit. You also need the proper paperwork from the military to apply for credit at a college. For the next steps to pursue, go to www.military.com. Click Education and College Credit for Service.

Date I'm going to start this first step: _____

Action: Apply for a Relevant Apprenticeship

First Step: Identify an Apprenticeship in Your Area

Once you know what kind of apprenticeship interests you, here are some resources for identifying programs in your area.

Places to Investigate Apprenticeships

- Union locals in your community
- Medium- to large-sized employers in your community

(continued)

(continued)

- Your state's Job Service (see the blue pages of your telephone book or www.jobbankinfo.org)
- A local One-Stop Career Center (see the blue pages of your telephone book)
- A school or college career counseling office
- A military recruitment office (see the blue pages of your telephone book), because some apprenticeships are offered as part of military training
- For people in the military (including the Reserves and the National Guard), the Transition Assistance Office or the Helmets to Hardhats program (http://helmetstohardhats.org/)
- Your state's office that registers apprenticeships. In some states, this is the State Apprenticeship Council (see the blue pages of your telephone book or www.doleta.gov/OA/stateagencies.cfm). In other states, it is the Bureau of Apprenticeship and Training (see the blue pages of your telephone book or www.doleta.gov/OA/stateoffices.cfm). Many states offer Web sites with searchable databases of apprenticeship programs.
- The searchable database of sponsors (who may or may not have apprenticeships open at present) at the Apprenticeship Training, Employer, and Labor Services Sponsors Web site (http://oa.doleta.gov/bat.cfm). Note that not all states are covered here and that listings on your state's own Web site may be more comprehensive or more current.

You may also find it useful to ask workers in the occupation that interests you, especially those who have recently completed an apprenticeship.

Date I'm going to start this first step: _____

Action: Apply to a Relevant Two- or Four-Year College Program

First Step: Identify a College Program

Two-year colleges usually try to match their programs to the needs of local employers. That means that if an occupation is in demand in your area, you can probably find a local college that offers an associate degree program for that job.

If you are planning for a four-year degree, you may already have a particular college in mind: maybe one in your community, maybe State U. If you don't have one in mind, a good first step is the college search at www.collegeboard.com. You can search by the majors that are offered, among other characteristics.

Once you have identified a likely institution, explore the Web site to be sure the college offers a program related to your career goal. Look at the requirements for the program—both for entry and for completion. Be sure that the content of the program is consistent with any career specialization you are planning for.

Next, call the department that offers the program and get answers to any questions that the Web site does not address. Be sure to ask about the job placement of recent graduates—specifically, the names of local employers that have hired graduates. Then phone supervisory people at these employers and ask whether they are satisfied with the skills of the graduates they have interviewed or hired—and, if not, whether there's another program that's better. (You'll find suggestions about how to contact local employers later in this chapter, in the section about making cold calls.)

Eventually, you're going to have to decide how to afford the expenses of college and whether you can find the time to attend. But those are later steps.

Date I'm going to start this first step: _____

Gap: You're Not Yet Ready to "Sell" Yourself

Bridge: Identifying and Documenting Your Brand

Action: Identify What Makes You Stand Out

First Step: Find Positive Language to Describe Yourself

Many people come from a background similar to yours, but there's only one you. To clarify your brand, fill in the blanks in the following section.

Exercises That Identify Your Brand

Assume that you just finished a job interview and left the room. The interviewer picks up the phone and says, "That person really _____
_____." What do you (realistically) want that interviewer to say?

Decide on three words that describe you best in a positive way:
A noun _____
An adjective _____
Another adjective _____

If you were to start a Web site that featured only your resume, what address would you use for your site? (Assume that you *can't use your name*.)
_____.com

Imagine that you're starting a business to sell your skills. What would you call the business? Use the model of Toys R Us and call it
_____ R Us or _____ —
That's Me. (Again, you *can't use your name*. Note that the "R Us" name is copyrighted, so you can't actually use it, but it's a good exercise for identifying your brand.)

Date I'm going to start this first step: _____

Action: Create Your Elevator Speech

First Step: Find a Concise Way to Describe Yourself

Your elevator speech is *not* your life story. It's not your job title. It's a very concise explanation of who you are and what your job goal is. To get started, fill in the blanks in the following section.

Ideas for Your Elevator Speech

My work-related goal is _____.

I'm looking for work because _____. (Note: If you have been fired or jailed or have some other negative reason, either skip this or find a positive way to express it. For example, some people say, "I'm looking for new opportunities.")

Something unique about me is _____. (Hint: Use ideas from the branding exercises in the previous section.)

A good example of how I benefited an employer is _____
_____. (Hint: Numbers—dollar figures or percentage increase of business—are very impressive here. Avoid industry jargon.)

These ideas aren't enough to finish your elevator speech. You're going to need to refine it and practice it until it becomes natural. But this is how to take a first step.

Date I'm going to start this first step: _____

Action: Focus Your Resume on Your Goal and Brand

First Step: Perfect the Objective Statement on Your Resume

Tailoring a resume is not a simple process, but a good first step is to use a statement of your objective. Not everyone uses an objective statement, but it can be helpful for making clear to your reader what your goal is.

Some people use the *noun-based* approach, starting with the name of something they are aiming at. Other information, such as key skills, may be included. Here are some examples:

Noun-Based Objective Statements

- Customer service manager in a large retail store.
- Web design position that utilizes my artistic and programming abilities.
- Advertising salesworker for a small-city television or radio station.
- An engineering technician position in a manufacturing setting where my excellent analytical and technical skills can improve processes and products.
- Elementary school teacher in a medium-size district.

Other people use the *verb-based* approach, starting with what they intend to do.

Verb-Based Objective Statements

- Produce videos for sales and training.
- Create marketing strategies for hotel chain.
- Edit content for a magazine or Web publication.
- Prepare tax documents and do other accounting tasks for small businesses.
- Design packaging for consumer products.

Remember that the objective statement does not, by itself, give a clear focus to your resume. But it's a first step.

Date I'm going to start this first step: _____

Gap: You Don't Know About Any Job Openings

Bridge: Finding the Hidden Job Market

Action: Inform Your Network

First Step: Identify Your Network

Make a list of everyone you know. You may want to organize the list into different groups, depending on the kind of connection you have (family, social, work, and so forth). Here are some examples of people to include.

Examples of Your Network

- Someone you went to school with years ago
- Someone you used to work with
- A relative you don't see very often
- The person who cuts your hair
- The parent of your child's soccer teammate
- The produce clerk in the supermarket
- Someone you see regularly at the gym
- Your doctor

- Your pet's veterinarian
- Your child's scout troop leader
- Someone in your faith group
- Someone in your neighborhood
- The real estate agent who sold you your house

Next, you'll let all these people know who you are—your brand—and the goal of your 2011 career plan. For now, your first step is just making this list.

Date I'm going to start this first step: _____

Action: Expand Your Network

First Step: Use Social Networking Web Sites

By now you've probably heard about LinkedIn.com, a Web site that's designed to help people network about work. If you import your address book to LinkedIn, the site will tell you which contacts have a LinkedIn profile and will alert you later when others sign up. LinkedIn also has a People You May Know page that shows you the contacts of your contacts; some of them may know you well enough to be willing to join your network. You can make this page retrieve additional names by clicking your browser's Reload or Refresh button.

LinkedIn has many helpful features for job-seekers, but they work only if you use them *actively*. Simply adding people to your network is only the first step; it will not make your contacts aware of your goal and what you have to offer.

Purely social sites such as Facebook and MySpace can also be useful, as long as you don't have anything on your page that employers would object to. As with LinkedIn, expand your network by looking for the contacts of your contacts.

Twitter is becoming a lively place for learning about job openings and building your network. By "following" people in your targeted industry, you can learn a lot about trends and perhaps about actual job openings. By "tweeting" about what you're doing and about industry news, you can help establish your brand. Remember that Twitter can help with your career only as long as you restrict your "tweets" to topics of professional interest.

For lots of useful suggestions, see *The Twitter Job Search Guide,* by Susan Britton Whitcomb, Chandlee Bryan, and Deb Dib (JIST).

Date I'm going to start this first step: _____

Action: Make Cold Calls

First Step: Identify Likely Employers

Remember, you use cold calls to contact employers regarding either their own job openings or job openings they may have heard about elsewhere. Either way, the most fruitful employers will be businesses that hire people for the kind of position you seek.

Ways to Identify Likely Employers

- Browse through business directories such as the Yellow Pages—or, on the Web, Yellowbook.com.

- Browse through the membership directory of your professional association and note which companies employ a lot of members.

- In the association's publications and conference programs, note which businesses sponsor the association or its activities.

- In magazines or Web sites aimed at your industry, note businesses that advertise there.

- Use the searchable Employer Locator database at the Career OneStop site: http://www.careerinfonet.org/employerlocator. This includes many small employers.

Date I'm going to start this first step: _____

Key Points: Chapter 5

- Your 2011 career plan has gaps that you need to bridge, but you can start with some easy first steps.

- To commit yourself fully to taking a first step, you need to set a date for starting it.

CHAPTER 6

Hang In There!

You're reading this chapter because your 2011 career goal is to increase your security in your present job. Or maybe you're looking ahead, wondering how you'll hang onto a job that you don't have yet.

You're right to be concerned about job security. During the worst months of the Great Recession, hundreds of thousands of workers were losing their jobs each month. We've moved past those dark days, but you're never going to see the kind of widespread job security that your grandparents came to expect during most of the previous century. Nowadays, very few employers feel any kind of loyalty toward their workers. When your work is no longer the best way to contribute to the company's bottom line, you're history. If your job can be done by a robot, a slick computer app, a worker on some foreign shore, a part-timer, a temporary worker, or a fresh-faced graduate with the latest book learning and low wage expectations—look out!

But take heart: I'll show you some steps you can take to make your job more secure.

Be the Irreplaceable Worker

The best way to hang onto your job is to be *irreplaceable*. You need to be so vital to the business that it can't go on without you. Here are some suggestions:

- **Focus on the core mission of the business.** Many businesses diversify and serve several functions, but usually there's a central mission that makes money and determines whether the business will succeed or fail. Identify that central function and play a role in it. Identify the skills the business needs for future development of this function and acquire them.

- **Be exceptionally productive.** This doesn't necessarily mean working longer hours. It's more important to find a task or role you can handle that goes beyond your job description. Here again, skills are important because they are the key to productivity.

- **Be visible.** In many businesses, the person whose office is next to the boss's tends to get the best performance appraisals. If you don't have that office, find ways to make your accomplishments known; don't wait for performance-appraisal season. For example, start an in-house Web page, newsletter, or bulletin board showcasing the project you're working on and soliciting suggestions from people outside the project. This will encourage them to buy into the project and make your efforts look not purely self-promotional. If you have a work-at-home arrangement, find reasons to show up at the office regularly or make lunch dates.

- **Acquire a mentor.** Find someone who really knows the business; be helpful; and ask a lot of very specific questions, including questions about how to improve your work. Give public credit to the mentor for the advice you get.

- **Be pleasant.** Back-stabbing may seem like a way to get ahead, but it can hurt you in the long run. Abrasiveness may make you stand out, but for the wrong reasons. If you really can't get along with some people in your work group, try to be transferred to one where you'll fit in better.

Be a Resilient Worker

For one reason or another, you may lose your job or get stuck in a dead-end job even while following the preceding tips. So the other strategy for keeping yourself employable is to *be resilient,* able to bounce back quickly. Here's how:

- **Specialize and focus on a specific goal.** After a few years in an occupation or industry, find a niche that is not overcrowded and is related to your core skills; then, acquire the specialized skills to excel in that role. In a tight job market, employers are more interested in someone with the perfect fit of skills than in a generalist. Your niche may be at the intersection of two very different skills; for example, you may be the chemist who is an ace computer programmer or the police officer who is an inspiring teacher.

- **Be visible beyond your workplace.** Join a professional organization, find something missing from their services, and put yourself in that key role. Start a blog or be active in commenting on a prominent blog; this is a readily available way to become known by people with connections in your industry. Start a Twitter feed that spreads news about your industry and specialization (and not where you went for lunch).

- **Keep your resume up to date.** Do more than list your current job title. Be sure to include a recent accomplishment so you don't look as though your career has been coasting. Make sure that your skills are easy to identify.

- **Keep your skills up to date.** The particular skills needed by your industry and for your targeted role will vary, but almost everybody needs to be familiar with productivity software such as spreadsheets.

- **Believe in yourself.** Every job you hold is just one scene in the drama that is your life. If one episode is going badly or ends suddenly, it doesn't have to turn the whole arc of your career into a tragedy. Instead, think of the setback as a plot complication or as an adventure.

When you rebound from a job loss, it may be into another job in the same occupation, or perhaps you'll be open to the idea of moving into another occupation in one of the hot fields. If you're considering the latter, turn to chapter 3 and start getting ideas about where you might find your next job.

Key Points: Chapter 6

- Job security faces many threats, even during the economic upturn after a recession.

- Workers with an essential job function, high productivity, and high visibility have the most job security.

- Job loss can happen to anyone, but resilient workers can bounce back.

Part II

Facts About the Hottest Jobs of 2011

All the jobs described here appear on at least one list in chapter 3. They were selected because they offer the most opportunity within the high-growth fields profiled in chapter 3: fast growth, moderate-to-high income, and a large workforce. Some of them show a great promise in several different fields; Accountants and Auditors, for example, appear on nine lists.

The appendix gives more details on how to use and interpret the job descriptions, but here are some important notes:

- Job descriptions are arranged in alphabetical order by job title. This approach allows you to quickly find a description if you know its correct title from one of the lists in chapter 3.

- If you are using this section to browse for interesting options, you may want to begin with the table of contents or with the fields listed in chapter 3.

- The economic information here represents national averages that apply across all industries. You may notice that some jobs here are slow-growing (or even shrinking) and others have rather low pay. However, every job here is fast-growing and well-paying *in at least one of the fields* discussed in chapter 2. Pay attention to the hot fields listed for each job; they are your best bets for your 2011 career plan.

Accountants

- Education/Training Required: Bachelor's degree
- Annual Earnings: $60,340
- Earnings Growth Potential: Medium
- Growth: 21.6%
- Annual Job Openings: 49,750
- Self-Employed: 8.1%

Our sources did not provide separate job openings data for this occupation. The job openings listed here are shared with Auditors.

Hottest Fields (with Growth): Management, Scientific, and Technical Consulting Services (92.6%); Computer Systems Design and Related Services (65.5%); Employment Services (38.9%); Software Publishers (32.8%); Scientific Research and Development Services (27.5%).

Analyze financial information and prepare financial reports to determine or maintain record of assets, liabilities, profit and loss, tax liability, or other financial activities within an organization. Prepare, examine, or analyze accounting records, financial statements, or other financial reports to assess accuracy, completeness, and conformance to reporting and procedural standards. Compute taxes owed and prepare tax returns, ensuring compliance with payment, reporting, or other tax requirements. Analyze business operations, trends, costs, revenues, financial commitments, and obligations to project future revenues and expenses or to provide advice. Report to management regarding the finances of establishment. Establish tables of accounts and assign entries to proper accounts. Develop, maintain, and analyze budgets, preparing periodic reports that compare budgeted costs to actual costs. Develop, implement, modify, and document recordkeeping and accounting systems, making use of current computer technology. Prepare forms and manuals for accounting and bookkeeping personnel and direct their work activities. Survey operations to ascertain accounting needs and to recommend, develop, or maintain solutions to business and financial problems. Provide internal and external auditing services for businesses or individuals. Advise clients in areas such as compensation, employee health-care benefits, the design of accounting or data processing systems, or long-range tax or estate plans. Investigate bankruptcies and other complex financial transactions and prepare reports summarizing the findings. Represent clients before taxing authorities and provide support during litigation involving financial issues.

Career Cluster: 04 Business, Management, and Administration. **Pathway:** 04.2 Business, Financial Management, and Accounting.

Personality Type: Conventional-Enterprising. **Skills:** Management of Financial Resources; Systems Analysis; Systems Evaluation; Operations Analysis; Judgment and Decision Making; Programming; Mathematics; Time Management.

Education/Training Programs: Accounting; Accounting and Business/ Management; Accounting and Computer Science; Accounting and Finance; Auditing; Taxation. **Related Knowledge/Courses:** Economics and Accounting; Clerical; Mathematics; Computers and Electronics; Personnel and Human Resources; Administration and Management.

Accountants and Auditors

See Accountants and Auditors, described separately.

Auditors

- Education/Training Required: Bachelor's degree
- Annual Earnings: $60,340
- Earnings Growth Potential: Medium
- Growth: 21.6%
- Annual Job Openings: 49,750
- Self-Employed: 8.1%

Our sources did not provide separate job openings data for this occupation. The job openings listed here are shared with Accountants.

Hottest Fields (with Growth): Management, Scientific, and Technical Consulting Services (92.6%); Computer Systems Design and Related Services (65.5%); Employment Services (38.9%); Software Publishers (32.8%); Scientific Research and Development Services (27.5%).

Examine and analyze accounting records to determine financial status of establishment and prepare financial reports concerning operating procedures. Collect and analyze data to detect deficient controls; duplicated effort; extravagance; fraud; or non-compliance with laws, regulations, and management policies. Prepare detailed reports on audit findings. Supervise auditing of establishments and determine scope of investigation required. Report to management about asset utilization and audit results and recommend changes in operations and financial activities. Inspect account books and accounting systems for efficiency, effectiveness, and use of accepted accounting procedures to record transactions. Examine records and interview workers to ensure recording of transactions and compliance with laws and regulations. Examine and evaluate financial and information systems, recommending controls to ensure system reliability and data integrity. Review data about material assets, net worth, liabilities, capital stock, surplus, income, and expenditures. Confer with company officials about financial and regulatory matters. Examine whether the organization's objectives are reflected in its management activities and whether employees understand the objectives. Prepare, analyze, and verify annual reports, financial statements, and other records, using accepted accounting and statistical procedures to assess financial condition and facilitate financial planning. Inspect cash on hand, notes receivable and payable, negotiable securities, and canceled checks to confirm records are accurate. Examine inventory to verify journal and ledger entries. Audit payroll and personnel records to determine unemployment insurance premiums, workers' compensation coverage, liabilities, and compliance with tax laws. Evaluate taxpayer finances to determine tax liability, using knowledge of interest and discount rates, annuities, valuation of stocks and bonds, and amortization valuation of depletable assets. Review taxpayer accounts and conduct audits on-site, by correspondence, or by summoning taxpayers to office.

Career Cluster: 04 Business, Management, and Administration. **Pathway:** 04.2 Business, Financial Management, and Accounting.

Personality Type: Conventional-Enterprising-Investigative. **Skills:** Systems Analysis; Systems Evaluation; Management of Personnel Resources; Writing; Management of Financial Resources; Persuasion; Speaking; Mathematics; Negotiation.

Education/Training Programs: Accounting; Accounting and Business/ Management; Accounting and Computer Science; Accounting and Finance; Auditing; Taxation. **Related Knowledge/Courses:** Economics and Accounting; Administration and Management; Personnel and Human Resources; Law and Government; Computers and Electronics; Mathematics.

Biochemists and Biophysicists

- Education/Training Required: Doctoral degree
- Annual Earnings: $82,390
- Earnings Growth Potential: High
- Growth: 37.4%
- Annual Job Openings: 1,620
- Self-Employed: 2.7%

Hottest Fields (with Growth): Management, Scientific, and Technical Consulting Services (123.3%); Scientific Research and Development Services (50.6%); Health Care (45.5%); Wholesale Trade (44.6%); Educational Services (34.4%).

Study the chemical composition and physical principles of living cells and organisms and their electrical and mechanical energy and related phenomena. May conduct research in order to further understanding of the complex chemical combinations and reactions involved in metabolism, reproduction, growth, and heredity. May determine the effects of foods, drugs, serums, hormones, and other substances on tissues and vital processes of living organisms. Design and perform experiments with equipment such as lasers, accelerators, and mass spectrometers. Analyze brain functions, such as learning, thinking, and memory, and analyze the dynamics of seeing and hearing. Share research findings by writing scientific articles and by making presentations at scientific conferences. Develop and test new drugs and medications intended for commercial distribution. Develop methods to process, store, and use foods, drugs, and chemical compounds. Develop new methods to study the mechanisms of biological processes. Examine the molecular and chemical aspects of immune system functioning. Investigate the nature, composition, and expression of genes and research how genetic engineering can impact these processes. Prepare reports and recommendations based upon research outcomes. Design and build laboratory equipment needed for special research projects. Isolate, analyze, and synthesize vitamins, hormones, allergens, minerals, and enzymes and determine their effects on body functions. Research cancer treatment, using radiation and nuclear particles. Research transformations of substances in cells, using atomic isotopes. Study spatial configurations of submicroscopic molecules such as proteins, using X rays and electron microscopes. Teach and advise undergraduate and graduate students and supervise their research. Investigate the transmission of electrical impulses along nerves and muscles. Research how characteristics of plants and animals are carried through successive generations. Investigate damage to cells and tissues caused by X rays and nuclear particles. Research the chemical effects of substances such as drugs, serums, hormones, and food on tissues and vital processes. Develop and execute tests to detect diseases, genetic disorders, or other abnormalities. Produce pharmaceutically and industrially useful proteins, using recombinant DNA technology.

Career Clusters: 01 Agriculture, Food, and Natural Resources; 15 Science, Technology, Engineering, and Mathematics. **Pathways:** 01.2 Plant Systems; 15.3 Science and Mathematics.

Personality Type: Investigative-Artistic-Realistic. **Skills:** Science; Technology Design; Writing; Operations Analysis; Equipment Selection; Reading Comprehension; Troubleshooting; Quality Control Analysis.

Education/Training Programs: Biochemistry; Biochemistry and Molecular Biology; Biophysics; Cell/Cellular Biology and Anatomical Sciences, Other; Molecular Biochemistry; Molecular Biophysics; Soil Chemistry and Physics; Soil Microbiology. **Related Knowledge/Courses:** No data available.

Biomedical Engineers

- Education/Training Required: Bachelor's degree
- Annual Earnings: $78,860
- Earnings Growth Potential: Medium
- Growth: 72.0%
- Annual Job Openings: 1,490
- Self-Employed: 3.3%

Hottest Fields (with Growth): Scientific Research and Development Services (90.4%); Health Care (71.8%); Computer and Electronic Product Manufacturing

(68.6%); Educational Services (68.1%); Pharmaceutical and Medicine Manufacturing (57.7%).

Apply knowledge of engineering, biology, and biomechanical principles to the design, development, and evaluation of biological and health systems and products, such as artificial organs, prostheses, instrumentation, medical information systems, and health management and care delivery systems. Evaluate the safety, efficiency, and effectiveness of biomedical equipment. Install, adjust, maintain, and/or repair biomedical equipment. Advise hospital administrators on the planning, acquisition, and use of medical equipment. Advise and assist in the application of instrumentation in clinical environments. Develop models or computer simulations of human bio-behavioral systems in order to obtain data for measuring or controlling life processes. Research new materials to be used for products such as implanted artificial organs. Design and develop medical diagnostic and clinical instrumentation, equipment, and procedures, utilizing the principles of engineering and bio-behavioral sciences. Conduct research, along with life scientists, chemists, and medical scientists, on the engineering aspects of the biological systems of humans and animals. Teach biomedical engineering or disseminate knowledge about field through writing or consulting. Design and deliver technology to assist people with disabilities. Diagnose and interpret bioelectric data, using signal-processing techniques. Adapt or design computer hardware or software for medical science uses.

Career Cluster: 15 Science, Technology, Engineering, and Mathematics. **Pathway:** 15.1 Engineering and Technology.

Personality Type: Investigative-Realistic. **Skills:** Technology Design; Science; Installation; Operations Analysis; Quality Control Analysis; Systems Evaluation; Troubleshooting; Management of Material Resources; Mathematics; Systems Analysis.

Education/Training Program: Bioengineering and Biomedical Engineering. **Related Knowledge/Courses:** No data available.

Child, Family, and School Social Workers

- Education/Training Required: Bachelor's degree
- Annual Earnings: $39,960
- Earnings Growth Potential: Low
- Growth: 12.3%
- Annual Job Openings: 10,960
- Self-Employed: 2.2%

Hottest Fields (with Growth): Employment Services (27.3%); Social Assistance, Except Child Day Care (21.5%); Health Care (13.0%); Advocacy, Grantmaking, and Civic Organizations (12.1%); Child Day Care Services (12.0%).

Provide social services and assistance to improve the social and psychological functioning of children and their families and to maximize the family well-being and the academic functioning of children. May assist single parents, arrange adoptions, and find foster homes for abandoned or abused children. In schools, they address such problems as teenage pregnancy, misbehavior, and truancy. May also advise teachers on how to deal with problem children. Interview clients individually, in families, or in groups, assessing their situations, capabilities, and problems, to determine what services are required to meet their needs. Counsel individuals, groups, families, or communities regarding issues including mental health, poverty, unemployment, substance abuse, physical abuse, rehabilitation, social adjustment, child care, or medical care. Maintain case history records and prepare reports. Counsel students whose behavior, school progress, or mental or physical impairment indicate a need for assistance, diagnosing students' problems and arranging for needed services. Consult with parents, teachers, and other school personnel to determine causes of problems such as truancy and misbehavior and to implement solutions. Counsel parents with child rearing problems, interviewing the child and family to determine whether further action is required. Develop and review service plans in consultation with clients and perform follow-ups assessing the quantity and quality of services provided. Collect supplementary information needed to assist clients, such as employment records, medical records, or school reports. Address legal issues, such as child abuse and discipline, assisting with hearings and providing testimony to inform custody arrangements. Provide, find, or arrange for support services, such as child care, homemaker service, prenatal care, substance abuse treatment, job training, counseling, or parenting classes, to prevent more serious problems from developing. Refer clients to community resources for services such as job placement, debt counseling, legal aid, housing, medical treatment, or financial assistance and provide concrete information, such as where to go and how to apply. Arrange for medical, psychiatric, and other tests that may disclose causes of difficulties and indicate remedial measures. Work in child and adolescent residential institutions. Administer welfare programs. Evaluate personal characteristics and home conditions of foster home or adoption applicants. Serve as liaisons between students, homes, schools, family services, child guidance clinics, courts, protective services, doctors, and other contacts to help children who face problems such as disabilities, abuse, or poverty.

Career Clusters: 10 Human Services; 12 Law, Public Safety, Corrections, and Security. **Pathways:** 10.3 Family and Community Services; 12.1 Correction Services.

Personality Type: Social-Enterprising. **Skills:** Social Perceptiveness; Service Orientation; Speaking; Monitoring; Writing; Learning Strategies; Negotiation; Active Listening.

Education/Training Programs: Juvenile Corrections; Social Work; Youth Services/Administration. **Related Knowledge/Courses:** No data available.

Coaches and Scouts

- Education/Training Required: Long-term on-the-job training
- Annual Earnings: $28,380
- Earnings Growth Potential: High
- Growth: 24.8%
- Annual Job Openings: 9,920
- Self-Employed: 16.2%

Hottest Fields (with Growth): Employment Services (38.1%); Social Assistance, Except Child Day Care (32.5%); Educational Services (29.4%); Advocacy, Grantmaking, and Civic Organizations (24.2%); Arts, Entertainment, and Recreation (21.6%).

Instruct or coach groups or individuals in the fundamentals of sports. Demonstrate techniques and methods of participation. May evaluate athletes' strengths and weaknesses as possible recruits or to improve the athletes' technique to prepare them for competition. Plan, organize, and conduct practice sessions. Provide training direction, encouragement, and motivation to prepare athletes for games, competitive events, or tours. Identify and recruit potential athletes, arranging and offering incentives such as athletic scholarships. Plan strategies and choose team members for individual games or sports seasons. Plan and direct physical conditioning programs that will enable athletes to achieve maximum performance. Adjust coaching techniques based on the strengths and weaknesses of athletes. File scouting reports that detail player assessments, provide recommendations on athlete recruitment, and identify locations and individuals to be targeted for future recruitment efforts. Keep records of athlete, team, and opposing team performance. Instruct individuals or groups in sports rules, game strategies, and performance principles such as specific ways of moving the body, hands, and feet in order to achieve desired results. Analyze the strengths and weaknesses of opposing teams to develop game strategies. Evaluate athletes' skills and review performance records to determine their fitness and potential in a particular area of athletics. Keep abreast of changing rules, techniques, technologies, and philosophies relevant to their sport. Monitor athletes' use of equipment to ensure safe and proper use. Explain and enforce safety rules and regulations. Develop and arrange competition schedules and programs. Serve as organizer, leader, instructor, or referee for outdoor and indoor games such as volleyball, football, and soccer. Explain and demonstrate the use of sports and training equipment, such as trampolines or weights. Perform activities that support a team or a specific sport, such as meeting with media representatives and appearing at fundraising events. Arrange and conduct sports-related activities such as training camps, skill-improvement courses, clinics, or pre-season try-outs.

Career Cluster: 05 Education and Training. **Pathways:** 05.1 Administration and Administrative Support; 05.3 Teaching/Training.

Personality Type: Social-Realistic-Enterprising. **Skills:** Social Perceptiveness; Management of Personnel Resources; Management of Financial Resources; Persuasion; Negotiation; Instructing; Monitoring; Time Management.

Education/Training Programs: Health and Physical Education, General; Physical Education Teaching and Coaching; Sport and Fitness Administration/ Management. **Related Knowledge/Courses:** Psychology; Therapy and Counseling; Education and Training; Sales and Marketing; Personnel and Human Resources; Sociology and Anthropology.

Compensation, Benefits, and Job Analysis Specialists

- Education/Training Required: Bachelor's degree
- Annual Earnings: $55,620
- Earnings Growth Potential: Medium
- Growth: 23.6%
- Annual Job Openings: 6,050
- Self-Employed: 1.6%

Hottest Fields (with Growth): Management, Scientific, and Technical Consulting Services (102.1%); Computer Systems Design and Related Services (59.8%); Social Assistance, Except Child Day Care (46.6%); Clothing, Accessory, and General Merchandise Stores (44.1%); Software Publishers (43.8%)

Conduct programs of compensation and benefits and job analysis for employer. May specialize in specific areas, such as position classification and pension programs. Evaluate job positions, determining classification, exempt or non-exempt status, and salary. Ensure company compliance with federal and state laws, including reporting requirements. Advise managers and employees on state and federal employment regulations, collective agreements, benefit and compensation policies, personnel procedures, and classification programs. Plan, develop, evaluate, improve, and communicate methods and techniques for selecting, promoting, compensating, evaluating, and training workers. Provide advice on the resolution of classification and salary complaints. Prepare occupational classifications, job descriptions, and salary scales. Assist in preparing and maintaining personnel records and handbooks. Prepare reports such as organization and flow charts and career path reports to summarize job analysis and evaluation and compensation analysis information. Administer employee insurance, pension, and savings plans, working with insurance brokers and plan carriers. Negotiate collective agreements on behalf of employers or workers and mediate labor disputes and grievances. Develop, implement, administer, and evaluate personnel and labor relations programs, including performance appraisal, affirmative action, and employment equity programs. Perform multifactor data and cost analyses that may be used in areas such as support of collective bargaining agreements. Research employee benefit and health and safety practices and recommend changes or modifications to existing policies. Analyze organizational, occupational, and industrial data to facilitate organizational functions and provide technical information to business, industry, and government. Advise staff of individuals' qualifications. Assess need for and develop job analysis instruments and materials.

Career Cluster: 04 Business, Management, and Administration. **Pathway:** 04.3 Human Resources.

Personality Type: Conventional-Enterprising. **Skills:** Service Orientation; Judgment and Decision Making; Management of Financial Resources; Persuasion; Active Listening; Negotiation; Monitoring; Coordination; Writing.

Education/Training Programs: Human Resources Management/Personnel Administration, General; Labor and Industrial Relations. **Related Knowledge/ Courses:** Personnel and Human Resources; Economics and Accounting; Law and Government; English Language; Administration and Management; Mathematics.

Compliance Officers, Except Agriculture, Construction, Health and Safety, and Transportation

See Coroners; Environmental Compliance Inspectors; Equal Opportunity Representatives and Officers; Government Property Inspectors and Investigators; and Licensing Examiners and Inspectors, described separately.

Computer and Information Systems Managers

- Education/Training Required: Work experience plus degree
- Annual Earnings: $113,720
- Earnings Growth Potential: Medium
- Growth: 16.9%
- Annual Job Openings: 9,710
- Self-Employed: 3.3%

Hottest Fields (with Growth): Management, Scientific, and Technical Consulting Services (83.9%); Computer Systems Design and Related Services (44.9%); Social Assistance, Except Child Day Care (34.1%); Software Publishers (30.3%); Health Care (29.0%).

Plan, direct, or coordinate activities in such fields as electronic data processing, information systems, systems analysis, and computer programming. Review project plans to plan and coordinate project activity. Manage backup, security, and user help systems. Develop and interpret organizational goals, policies, and procedures. Develop computer information resources, providing for data security and control, strategic computing, and disaster recovery. Consult with users, management, vendors, and technicians to assess computing needs and system requirements. Stay abreast of advances in technology. Meet with department heads, managers, supervisors, vendors, and others to solicit cooperation and resolve problems. Provide users with technical support for computer problems. Recruit, hire,

93

train, and supervise staff or participate in staffing decisions. Evaluate data processing proposals to assess project feasibility and requirements. Review and approve all systems charts and programs prior to their implementation. Control operational budget and expenditures. Direct daily operations of department, analyzing workflow, establishing priorities, developing standards, and setting deadlines. Assign and review the work of systems analysts, programmers, and other computer-related workers. Evaluate the organization's technology use and needs and recommend improvements such as hardware and software upgrades.

Career Clusters: 04 Business, Management, and Administration; 11 Information Technology. **Pathways:** 04.1 Management; 04.4 Business Analysis; 11.1 Network Systems; 11.2 Information Support Services.

Personality Type: Enterprising-Conventional-Investigative. **Skills:** Systems Evaluation; Programming; Systems Analysis; Management of Financial Resources; Management of Material Resources; Management of Personnel Resources; Operation Monitoring; Negotiation; Repairing.

Education/Training Programs: Computer and Information Sciences, General; Computer Science; Information Resources Management/CIO Training; Information Science/Studies; Knowledge Management; Management Information Systems, General; Network and System Administration/Administrator; Operations Management and Supervision. **Related Knowledge/Courses:** Telecommunications; Computers and Electronics; Economics and Accounting; Production and Processing; Personnel and Human Resources; Administration and Management.

Computer Security Specialists

- Education/Training Required: Bachelor's degree
- Annual Earnings: $67,710
- Earnings Growth Potential: Medium
- Growth: 23.2%
- Annual Job Openings: 13,550
- Self-Employed: 0.8%

Our sources did not provide separate job openings data for this occupation. The job openings listed here are shared with Network and Computer Systems Administrators.

Hottest Fields (with Growth): Management, Scientific, and Technical Consulting Services (83.8%); Computer Systems Design and Related Services (71.7%); Software Publishers (55.2%); Health Care (41.1%); Social Assistance, Except Child Day Care (29.7%).

Plan, coordinate, and implement security measures for information systems to regulate access to computer data files and prevent unauthorized modification, destruction, or disclosure of information. Train users and promote security awareness to ensure system security and to improve server and network efficiency. Develop plans to safeguard computer files against accidental or unauthorized modification, destruction, or disclosure and to meet emergency data processing needs. Confer with users to discuss issues such as computer data access needs, security violations, and programming changes. Monitor current reports of computer viruses to determine when to update virus protection systems. Modify computer security files to incorporate new software, correct errors, or change individual access status. Coordinate implementation of computer system plan with establishment personnel and outside vendors. Monitor use of data files and regulate access to safeguard information in computer files. Perform risk assessments and execute tests of data-processing system to ensure functioning of data-processing activities and security measures. Encrypt data transmissions and erect firewalls to conceal confidential information as it is being transmitted and to keep out tainted digital transfers. Document computer security and emergency measures policies, procedures, and tests. Review violations of computer security procedures and discuss procedures with violators to ensure violations are not repeated.

Career Cluster: 11 Information Technology. **Pathway:** 11.4 Programming and Software Development.

Personality Type: Conventional-Investigative-Realistic. **Skills:** Systems Evaluation; Systems Analysis; Operations Analysis; Programming; Installation; Management of Material Resources; Troubleshooting; Management of Financial Resources.

Education/Training Programs: Computer and Information Sciences and Support Services, Other; Computer and Information Sciences, General; Computer and Information Systems Security/Information Assurance; Computer Systems Analysis/Analyst; Computer Systems Networking and Telecommunications; Information Science/Studies; Network and System Administration/Administrator; System, Networking, and LAN/WAN Management/Manager. **Related Knowledge/Courses:** No data available.

Computer Software Engineers, Applications

- Education/Training Required: Bachelor's degree
- Annual Earnings: $87,480
- Earnings Growth Potential: Medium
- Growth: 34.0%
- Annual Job Openings: 21,840
- Self-Employed: 2.7%

Hottest Fields (with Growth): Management, Scientific, and Technical Consulting Services (102.4%); Computer Systems Design and Related Services (57.3%); Social Assistance, Except Child Day Care (42.9%); Scientific Research and Development Services (37.7%); Construction (34.1%).

Develop, create, and modify general computer applications software or specialized utility programs. Analyze user needs and develop software solutions. Design software or customize software for client use with the aim of optimizing operational efficiency. May analyze and design databases within an application area, working individually or coordinating database development as part of a team. Confer with systems analysts, engineers, programmers, and others to design system and to obtain information on project limitations and capabilities, performance requirements, and interfaces. Modify existing software to correct errors, allow it to adapt to new hardware, or improve its performance. Analyze user needs and software requirements to determine feasibility of design within time and cost constraints. Consult with customers about software system design and maintenance. Coordinate software system installation and monitor equipment functioning to ensure specifications are met. Design, develop, and modify software systems, using scientific analysis and mathematical models to predict and measure outcome and consequences of design. Develop and direct software system testing and validation procedures, programming, and documentation. Analyze information to determine, recommend, and plan computer specifications and layouts and peripheral equipment modifications. Supervise the work of programmers, technologists, and technicians and other engineering and scientific personnel. Obtain and evaluate information on factors such as reporting formats required, costs, and security needs to determine hardware configuration. Determine system performance standards. Train users to use new or modified equipment. Store, retrieve, and manipulate data for analysis of system capabilities and requirements.

Career Clusters: 11 Information Technology; 15 Science, Technology, Engineering, and Mathematics. **Pathways:** 11.1 Network Systems; 11.2 Information Support Services; 11.3 Interactive Media; 11.4 Programming and Software Development; 15.3 Science and Mathematics.

Personality Type: Investigative-Realistic-Conventional. **Skills:** Programming; Troubleshooting; Technology Design; Systems Analysis; Quality Control Analysis; Operations Analysis; Installation; Complex Problem Solving.

Education/Training Programs: Artificial Intelligence; Bioinformatics; Computer Engineering Technologies/Technicians, Other; Computer Engineering, General; Computer Science; Computer Software Engineering; Information Technology; Medical Illustration and Informatics, Other; Medical Informatics. **Related Knowledge/Courses:** No data available.

Computer Software Engineers, Systems Software

- Education/Training Required: Bachelor's degree
- Annual Earnings: $93,470
- Earnings Growth Potential: Medium
- Growth: 30.4%

- Annual Job Openings: 15,340
- Self-Employed: 2.7%

Hottest Fields (with Growth): Management, Scientific, and Technical Consulting Services (102.4%); Computer Systems Design and Related Services (57.4%); Construction (40.4%); Scientific Research and Development Services (37.8%); Employment Services (33.8%).

Research, design, develop, and test operating systems—level software, compilers, and network distribution software for medical, industrial, military, communications, aerospace, business, scientific, and general computing applications. Set operational specifications and formulate and analyze software requirements. Apply principles and techniques of computer science, engineering, and mathematical analysis. Modify existing software to correct errors, to adapt it to new hardware, or to upgrade interfaces and improve performance. Design and develop software systems, using scientific analysis and mathematical models to predict and measure outcome and consequences of design. Consult with engineering staff to evaluate interface between hardware and software, develop specifications and performance requirements, and resolve customer problems. Analyze information to determine, recommend, and plan installation of a new system or modification of an existing system. Develop and direct software system testing and validation procedures. Direct software programming and development of documentation. Consult with customers or other departments on project status, proposals, and technical issues such as software system design and maintenance. Advise customer about, or perform, maintenance of software system. Coordinate installation of software system. Monitor functioning of equipment to ensure system operates in conformance with specifications. Store, retrieve, and manipulate data for analysis of system capabilities and requirements. Confer with data processing and project managers to obtain information on limitations and capabilities for data-processing projects. Prepare reports and correspondence concerning project specifications, activities, and status. Evaluate factors such as reporting formats required, cost constraints, and need for security restrictions to determine hardware configuration. Supervise and assign work to programmers, designers, technologists and technicians, and other engineering and scientific personnel. Train users to use new or modified equipment.

Career Cluster: 11 Information Technology. **Pathways:** 11.1 Network Systems; 11.2 Information Support Services; 11.3 Interactive Media; 11.4 Programming and Software Development.

Personality Type: Investigative-Conventional-Realistic. **Skills:** Programming; Technology Design; Systems Analysis; Troubleshooting; Operations Analysis; Complex Problem Solving; Science; Mathematics.

Education/Training Programs: Artificial Intelligence; Computer Engineering Technologies/Technicians, Other; Computer Engineering, General; Computer

Science; Information Science/Studies; Information Technology. **Related Knowledge/Courses:** No data available.

Computer Support Specialists

- Education/Training Required: Associate degree
- Annual Earnings: $44,300
- Earnings Growth Potential: Medium
- Growth: 13.8%
- Annual Job Openings: 23,460
- Self-Employed: 1.2%

Hottest Fields (with Growth): Management, Scientific, and Technical Consulting Services (66.9%); Computer Systems Design and Related Services (57.4%); Software Publishers (42.2%); Employment Services (21.6%); Health Care (15.5%).

Provide technical assistance to computer system users. Answer questions or resolve computer problems for clients in person, via telephone, or from remote locations. May provide assistance concerning the use of computer hardware and software, including printing, installation, word processing, e-mail, and operating systems. Oversee the daily performance of computer systems. Answer user inquiries regarding computer software or hardware operation to resolve problems. Enter commands and observe system functioning to verify correct operations and detect errors. Set up equipment for employee use, performing or ensuring proper installation of cables, operating systems, or appropriate software. Install and perform minor repairs to hardware, software, or peripheral equipment, following design or installation specifications. Maintain records of daily data communication transactions, problems and remedial actions taken, or installation activities. Read technical manuals, confer with users, or conduct computer diagnostics to investigate and resolve problems or to provide technical assistance and support. Refer major hardware or software problems or defective products to vendors or technicians for service. Develop training materials and procedures or train users in the proper use of hardware or software. Confer with staff, users, and management to establish requirements for new systems or modifications. Prepare evaluations of software or hardware and recommend improvements or upgrades. Read trade magazines and technical manuals or attend conferences and seminars to maintain knowledge of hardware and software. Hire, supervise, and direct workers engaged in special project work, problem solving, monitoring, and installing data communication equipment and software.

Career Clusters: 01 Agriculture, Food, and Natural Resources; 08 Health Science; 11 Information Technology; 13 Manufacturing; 15 Science, Technology, Engineering, and Mathematics. **Pathways:** 01.1 Food Products and Processing Systems; 08.3 Health Informatics; 11.2 Information Support Services; 13.3 Maintenance, Installation, and Repair; 15.3 Science and Mathematics.

Personality Type: Realistic-Investigative-Conventional. **Skills:** Systems Analysis; Operation Monitoring; Quality Control Analysis; Systems Evaluation; Repairing.

Education/Training Programs: Accounting and Computer Science; Agricultural Business Technology; Computer Hardware Technology/Technician; Computer Software Technology/Technician; Data Processing and Data Processing Technology/Technician; Medical Office Computer Specialist/Assistant Training. **Related Knowledge/Courses:** No data available.

Computer Systems Analysts

- Education/Training Required: Bachelor's degree
- Annual Earnings: $77,080
- Earnings Growth Potential: Medium
- Growth: 20.3%
- Annual Job Openings: 22,280
- Self-Employed: 5.7%

Our sources did not provide separate job openings data for this occupation. The job openings listed here are shared with Informatics Nurse Specialists.

Hottest Fields (with Growth): Management, Scientific, and Technical Consulting Services (85.4%); Software Publishers (42.3%); Computer Systems Design and Related Services (40.2%); Health Care (28.5%); Scientific Research and Development Services (24.7%).

Analyze science, engineering, business, and all other data-processing problems for application to electronic data-processing systems. Analyze user requirements, procedures, and problems to automate or improve existing systems and review computer system capabilities, workflow, and scheduling limitations. May analyze or recommend commercially available software. May supervise computer programmers. Provide staff and users with assistance solving computer-related problems, such as malfunctions and program problems. Test, maintain, and monitor computer programs and systems, including coordinating the installation of computer programs and systems. Use object-oriented programming languages as well as client and server applications development processes and multimedia and Internet technology. Confer with clients regarding the nature of the information processing or computation needs a computer program is to address. Coordinate and link the computer systems within an organization to increase compatibility and so information can be shared. Consult with management to ensure agreement on system principles. Expand or modify system to serve new purposes or improve workflow. Interview or survey workers, observe job performance, or perform the job to determine what information is processed and how it is processed. Determine computer software or hardware needed to set up or alter system. Train staff and users to work with computer systems and programs. Analyze information processing or computation needs and plan and design computer systems, using techniques such as structured analysis, data modeling, and information engineering. Assess the usefulness of pre-developed application packages and adapt them to a user environment. Define the goals of the system and devise flow charts and diagrams describing logical operational steps of programs. Develop, document, and revise system design procedures, test procedures, and quality standards.

Career Cluster: 11 Information Technology. **Pathways:** 11.2 Information Support Services; 11.3 Interactive Media; 11.4 Programming and Software Development.

Personality Type: Investigative-Conventional-Realistic. **Skills:** Installation; Quality Control Analysis; Technology Design; Programming; Systems Analysis; Troubleshooting; Operations Analysis; Systems Evaluation.

Education/Training Programs: Computer and Information Sciences, General; Computer Systems Analysis/Analyst; Information Technology; Web/Multimedia Management and Webmaster. **Related Knowledge/Courses:** No data available.

Construction Laborers

- Education/Training Required: Moderate-term on-the-job training
- Annual Earnings: $29,150
- Earnings Growth Potential: Medium
- Growth: 20.5%
- Annual Job Openings: 33,940
- Self-Employed: 21.3%

Hottest Fields (with Growth): Management, Scientific, and Technical Consulting Services (80.6%); Employment Services (33.8%); Construction (25.6%); Scientific Research and Development Services (22.2%); Social Assistance, Except Child Day Care (18.9%).

Perform tasks involving physical labor at building, highway, and heavy construction projects; tunnel and shaft excavations; and demolition sites. May operate hand and power tools of all types: air hammers, earth tampers, cement mixers, small mechanical hoists, surveying and measuring equipment, and various other types of equipment and instruments. May clean and prepare sites; dig trenches; set braces to support the sides of excavations; erect scaffolding; clean up rubble and debris; and remove asbestos, lead, and other hazardous waste materials. May assist other craft workers. Clean and prepare construction sites to eliminate possible hazards. Read and interpret plans, instructions, and specifications to determine work activities. Control traffic passing near, in, and around work zones. Signal equipment operators to facilitate alignment, movement, and adjustment of machinery, equipment, and materials. Dig ditches or trenches, backfill excavations, and compact and level earth to grade specifications, using picks, shovels, pneumatic tampers, and rakes. Measure, mark, and record openings and distances to lay out areas where construction work will be performed. Position, join, align, and seal structural components, such as concrete wall sections and pipes. Load, unload, and identify building materials, machinery, and tools and distribute them to the appropriate locations according to project plans and specifications. Erect and disassemble scaffolding, shoring, braces, traffic barricades, ramps, and other temporary structures. Build and position forms for pouring concrete and dismantle forms after use, using saws, hammers, nails, or bolts. Lubricate, clean, and repair machinery, equipment, and tools. Operate jackhammers and drills to break up concrete or pavement. Install sewer, water, and storm drain pipes, using pipe-laying machinery and laser guidance equipment. Transport and set explosives for tunnel, shaft, and road construction. Provide assistance to craft workers, such as carpenters, plasterers, and masons. Tend pumps, compressors, and generators to provide power for tools, machinery, and equipment or to heat and move materials such as asphalt. Mop, brush, or spread paints, cleaning solutions, or other compounds over surfaces to clean them or to provide protection.

Career Cluster: 02 Architecture and Construction. **Pathway:** 02.2 Construction.

Personality Type: Realistic-Conventional. **Skills:** Equipment Maintenance; Repairing; Equipment Selection; Installation.

Education/Training Program: Construction Trades, Other. **Related Knowledge/ Courses:** Building and Construction; Design; Mechanical; Transportation; Engineering and Technology; Public Safety and Security.

Coroners

- Education/Training Required: Work experience in a related occupation
- Annual Earnings: $49,750
- Earnings Growth Potential: Medium
- Growth: 31.0%
- Annual Job Openings: 10,850
- Self-Employed: 1.4%

Our sources did not provide separate job openings data for this occupation. The job openings listed here are shared with Environmental Compliance Inspectors; Equal Opportunity Representatives and Officers; Government Property Inspectors and Investigators; Licensing Examiners and Inspectors; and Regulatory Affairs Specialists.

Hottest Fields (with Growth): Management, Scientific, and Technical Consulting Services (120.9%); Computer Systems Design and Related Services (71.4%); Software Publishers (57.7%); Social Assistance, Except Child Day Care (54.6%); Scientific Research and Development Services (49.9%).

Direct activities such as autopsies, pathological and toxicological analyses, and inquests relating to the investigation of deaths occurring within a legal

jurisdiction to determine cause of death or to fix responsibility for accidental, violent, or unexplained deaths. Perform medico-legal examinations and autopsies, conducting preliminary examinations of the body in order to identify victims, to locate signs of trauma, and to identify factors that would indicate time of death. Inquire into the cause, manner, and circumstances of human deaths and establish the identities of deceased persons. Direct activities of workers who conduct autopsies, perform pathological and toxicological analyses, and prepare documents for permanent records. Complete death certificates, including the assignment of a cause and manner of death. Observe and record the positions and conditions of bodies and of related evidence. Collect and document any pertinent medical history information. Observe, record, and preserve any objects or personal property related to deaths, including objects such as medication containers and suicide notes. Complete reports and forms required to finalize cases. Remove or supervise removal of bodies from death scenes, using the proper equipment and supplies, and arrange for transportation to morgues. Testify at inquests, hearings, and court trials. Interview persons present at death scenes to obtain information useful in determining the manner of death. Provide information concerning the circumstances of death to relatives of the deceased. Locate and document information regarding the next of kin, including their relationship to the deceased and the status of notification attempts. Confer with officials of public health and law enforcement agencies in order to coordinate interdepartmental activities. Inventory personal effects, such as jewelry or wallets, that are recovered from bodies. Coordinate the release of personal effects to authorized persons and facilitate the disposition of unclaimed corpses and personal effects. Arrange for the next of kin to be notified of deaths. Record the disposition of minor children, as well as details of arrangements made for their care.

Career Cluster: 12 Law, Public Safety, Corrections, and Security. **Pathway:** 12.6 Inspection Services.

Personality Type: Investigative-Realistic-Conventional. **Skills:** Science; Management of Financial Resources; Reading Comprehension; Critical Thinking; Management of Personnel Resources; Speaking; Management of Material Resources; Writing.

Education/Training Program: Public Administration. **Related Knowledge/ Courses:** Medicine and Dentistry; Biology; Psychology; Therapy and Counseling; Chemistry; Law and Government.

Cost Estimators

- Education/Training Required: Bachelor's degree
- Annual Earnings: $57,300
- Earnings Growth Potential: High
- Growth: 25.3%

- Annual Job Openings: 10,360
- Self-Employed: 2.0%

Hottest Fields (with Growth): Management, Scientific, and Technical Consulting Services (102.6%); Computer Systems Design and Related Services (56.9%); Scientific Research and Development Services (38.3%); Employment Services (33.9%); Construction (33.1%).

Prepare cost estimates for product manufacturing, construction projects, or services to aid management in bidding on or determining prices of products or services. May specialize according to particular service performed or type of product manufactured. Consult with clients, vendors, personnel in other departments, or construction foremen to discuss and formulate estimates and resolve issues. Analyze blueprints and other documentation to prepare time, cost, materials, and labor estimates. Prepare estimates for use in selecting vendors or subcontractors. Confer with engineers, architects, owners, contractors, and sub-contractors on changes and adjustments to cost estimates. Prepare estimates used by management for purposes such as planning, organizing, and scheduling work. Prepare cost and expenditure statements and other necessary documentation at regular intervals for the duration of the project. Assess cost-effectiveness of products, projects, or services, tracking actual costs relative to bids as projects develop. Set up cost-monitoring and cost-reporting systems and procedures. Conduct special studies to develop and establish standard hour and related cost data or to effect cost reductions. Review material and labor requirements to decide whether it is more cost-effective to produce or purchase components. Prepare and maintain a directory of suppliers, contractors, and subcontractors.

Career Clusters: 02 Architecture and Construction; 04 Business, Management, and Administration; 13 Manufacturing; 15 Science, Technology, Engineering, and Mathematics. **Pathways:** 02.2 Construction; 04.1 Management; 13.1 Production; 15.1 Engineering and Technology.

Personality Type: Conventional-Enterprising. **Skills:** Management of Financial Resources; Systems Analysis; Management of Material Resources; Mathematics; Systems Evaluation; Persuasion; Complex Problem Solving; Negotiation.

Education/Training Programs: Business Administration and Management, General; Business/Commerce, General; Construction Engineering; Construction Engineering Technology/Technician; Manufacturing Engineering; Materials Engineering; Mechanical Engineering. **Related Knowledge/Courses:** Engineering and Technology; Mathematics; Economics and Accounting; Building and Construction; Design; Computers and Electronics.

Customer Service Representatives

- Education/Training Required: Moderate-term on-the-job training
- Annual Earnings: $30,290

- Earnings Growth Potential: Low
- Growth: 17.7%
- Annual Job Openings: 110,840
- Self-Employed: 0.4%

Our sources did not provide separate job openings data for this occupation. The job openings listed here are shared with Patient Representatives.

Hottest Fields (with Growth): Management, Scientific, and Technical Consulting Services (104.0%); Educational Services (44.7%); Computer Systems Design and Related Services (43.0%); Software Publishers (41.2%); Employment Services (35.9%).

Interact with customers to provide information in response to inquiries about products and services and to handle and resolve complaints. Confer with customers by telephone or in person to provide information about products and services, to take orders or cancel accounts, or to obtain details of complaints. Keep records of customer interactions and transactions, recording details of inquiries, complaints, and comments, as well as actions taken. Resolve customers' service or billing complaints by performing activities such as exchanging merchandise, refunding money, and adjusting bills. Check to ensure that appropriate changes were made to resolve customers' problems. Contact customers to respond to inquiries or to notify them of claim investigation results and any planned adjustments. Refer unresolved customer grievances to designated departments for further investigation. Determine charges for services requested, collect deposits or payments, or arrange for billing. Complete contract forms, prepare change of address records, and issue service discontinuance orders, using computers. Obtain and examine all relevant information to assess validity of complaints and to determine possible causes, such as extreme weather conditions, that could increase utility bills. Solicit sale of new or additional services or products. Review claims adjustments with dealers, examining parts claimed to be defective and approving or disapproving dealers' claims. Compare disputed merchandise with original requisitions and information from invoices and prepare invoices for returned goods.

Career Cluster: 04 Business, Management, and Administration. **Pathway:** 04.6 Administrative and Information Support.

Personality Type: Enterprising-Social-Conventional. **Skills:** Service Orientation; Monitoring; Reading Comprehension; Active Listening; Social Perceptiveness.

Education/Training Programs: Customer Service Support/Call Center/ Teleservice Operation; Receptionist Training. **Related Knowledge/Courses:** Clerical; Customer and Personal Service; English Language.

Database Administrators

- Education/Training Required: Bachelor's degree
- Annual Earnings: $71,550
- Earnings Growth Potential: High
- Growth: 20.3%
- Annual Job Openings: 4,440
- Self-Employed: 0.6%

Hottest Fields (with Growth): Management, Scientific, and Technical Consulting Services (83.6%); Computer Systems Design and Related Services (57.3%); Health Care (46.1%); Software Publishers (42.2%); Social Assistance, Except Child Day Care (29.8%).

Coordinate changes to computer databases. Test and implement the databases, applying knowledge of database management systems. May plan, coordinate, and implement security measures to safeguard computer databases. Test programs or databases, correct errors, and make necessary modifications. Modify existing databases and database management systems or direct programmers and analysts to make changes. Plan, coordinate, and implement security measures to safeguard information in computer files against accidental or unauthorized damage, modification, or disclosure. Work as part of project teams to coordinate database development and determine project scope and limitations. Write and code logical and physical database descriptions and specify identifiers of database to management system or direct others in coding descriptions. Train users and answer questions. Specify users and user access levels for each segment of databases. Approve, schedule, plan, and supervise the installation and testing of new products and improvements to computer systems such as the installation of new databases. Review project requests describing database user needs to estimate time and cost required to accomplish project. Review procedures in database management system manuals for making changes to database. Develop methods for integrating different products so they work properly together such as customizing commercial databases to fit specific needs. Develop data models describing data elements and how they are used, following procedures and using pen, template, or computer software. Select and enter codes to monitor database performances and to create production databases. Establish and calculate optimum values for database parameters, using manuals and calculators.

Career Clusters: 04 Business, Management, and Administration; 11 Information Technology. **Pathways:** 04.4 Business Analysis; 11.2 Information Support Services; 11.4 Programming and Software Development.

Personality Type: Conventional-Investigative. **Skills:** Programming; Systems Analysis; Systems Evaluation; Management of Personnel Resources; Operation Monitoring; Complex Problem Solving; Troubleshooting; Judgment and Decision Making.

Education/Training Programs: Computer and Information Sciences, General; Computer and Information Systems Security/Information Assurance; Computer Systems Analysis/Analyst; Data Modeling/Warehousing and Database Administration; Management Information Systems, General. **Related Knowledge/Courses:** No data available.

Dental Assistants

- Education/Training Required: Moderate-term on-the-job training
- Annual Earnings: $33,230
- Earnings Growth Potential: Low
- Growth: 35.7%
- Annual Job Openings: 16,100
- Self-Employed: 0.0%

Hottest Fields (with Growth): Management, Scientific, and Technical Consulting Services (84.2%); Health Care (36.8%); Employment Services (23.8%); Social Assistance, Except Child Day Care (16.1%); Educational Services (12.5%).

Assist dentist, set up patient and equipment, and keep records. Prepare patient, sterilize and disinfect instruments, set up instrument trays, prepare materials, and assist dentist during dental procedures. Expose dental diagnostic X rays. Record treatment information in patient records. Take and record medical and dental histories and vital signs of patients. Provide postoperative instructions prescribed by dentist. Assist dentist in management of medical and dental emergencies. Pour, trim, and polish study casts. Instruct patients in oral hygiene and plaque control programs. Make preliminary impressions for study casts and occlusal registrations for mounting study casts. Clean and polish removable appliances. Clean teeth, using dental instruments. Apply protective coating of fluoride to teeth. Fabricate temporary restorations and custom impressions from preliminary impressions. Schedule appointments, prepare bills, and receive payment for dental services; complete insurance forms; and maintain records, manually or using computer.

Career Cluster: 08 Health Science. **Pathway:** 08.1 Therapeutic Services.

Personality Type: Conventional-Realistic-Social. **Skills:** Equipment Maintenance; Operation and Control; Social Perceptiveness; Management of Material Resources; Operation Monitoring; Equipment Selection; Installation; Repairing.

Education/Training Program: Dental Assisting/Assistant. **Related Knowledge/Courses:** Medicine and Dentistry; Customer and Personal Service; Psychology; Sales and Marketing.

Dental Hygienists

- Education/Training Required: Associate degree
- Annual Earnings: $67,340

- Earnings Growth Potential: Low
- Growth: 36.1%
- Annual Job Openings: 9,840
- Self-Employed: 0.1%

Hottest Fields (with Growth): Management, Scientific, and Technical Consulting Services (78.9%); Health Care (36.7%); Employment Services (22.3%); Social Assistance, Except Child Day Care (18.8%); Educational Services (10.8%).

Clean teeth and examine oral areas, head, and neck for signs of oral disease. May educate patients on oral hygiene, take and develop X rays, or apply fluoride or sealants. Clean calcareous deposits, accretions, and stains from teeth and beneath margins of gums, using dental instruments. Feel and visually examine gums for sores and signs of disease. Chart conditions of decay and disease for diagnosis and treatment by dentist. Feel lymph nodes under patient's chin to detect swelling or tenderness that could indicate presence of oral cancer. Apply fluorides and other cavity-preventing agents to arrest dental decay. Examine gums, using probes, to locate periodontal recessed gums and signs of gum disease. Expose and develop X-ray film. Provide clinical services and health education to improve and maintain oral health of schoolchildren. Remove excess cement from coronal surfaces of teeth. Make impressions for study casts. Place, carve, and finish amalgam restorations. Administer local anesthetic agents. Conduct dental health clinics for community groups to augment services of dentist. Remove sutures and dressings. Place and remove rubber dams, matrices, and temporary restorations.

Career Cluster: 08 Health Science. **Pathway:** 08.1 Therapeutic Services.

Personality Type: Social-Realistic-Conventional. **Skills:** Active Learning; Science; Reading Comprehension; Time Management; Equipment Selection; Persuasion; Social Perceptiveness; Writing.

Education/Training Program: Dental Hygiene/Hygienist. **Related Knowledge/Courses:** Medicine and Dentistry; Psychology; Therapy and Counseling; Chemistry; Biology; Sales and Marketing.

Editors

- Education/Training Required: Bachelor's degree
- Annual Earnings: $50,800
- Earnings Growth Potential: High
- Growth: –0.3%
- Annual Job Openings: 3,390
- Self-Employed: 12.1%

Hottest Fields (with Growth): Management, Scientific, and Technical Consulting Services (86.7%); Computer Systems Design and Related Services (40.8%);

Software Publishers (29.6%); Arts, Entertainment, and Recreation (26.6%); Employment Services (24.1%).

Perform variety of editorial duties, such as laying out, indexing, and revising content of written materials, in preparation for final publication. Prepare, rewrite, and edit copy to improve readability or supervise others who do this work. Read copy or proof to detect and correct errors in spelling, punctuation, and syntax. Allocate print space for story text, photos, and illustrations according to space parameters and copy significance, using knowledge of layout principles. Plan the contents of publications according to the publication's style, editorial policy, and publishing requirements. Verify facts, dates, and statistics, using standard reference sources. Review and approve proofs submitted by composing room prior to publication production. Develop story or content ideas, considering reader or audience appeal. Oversee publication production, including artwork, layout, computer typesetting, and printing, ensuring adherence to deadlines and budget requirements. Confer with management and editorial staff members regarding placement and emphasis of developing news stories. Assign topics, events, and stories to individual writers or reporters for coverage. Read, evaluate, and edit manuscripts or other materials submitted for publication and confer with authors regarding changes in content, style or organization, or publication. Monitor news-gathering operations to ensure utilization of all news sources, such as press releases, telephone contacts, radio, television, wire services, and other reporters. Meet frequently with artists, typesetters, layout personnel, marketing directors, and production managers to discuss projects and resolve problems. Supervise and coordinate work of reporters and other editors. Make manuscript acceptance or revision recommendations to the publisher. Select local, state, national, and international news items received from wire services based on assessment of items' significance and interest value. Interview and hire writers and reporters or negotiate contracts, royalties, and payments for authors or freelancers. Direct the policies and departments of newspapers, magazines, and other publishing establishments.

Career Cluster: 03 Arts, Audio/Video Technology, and Communications. **Pathway:** 03.5 Journalism and Broadcasting.

Personality Type: Artistic-Enterprising-Conventional. **Skills:** Writing; Reading Comprehension; Active Listening; Judgment and Decision Making; Critical Thinking; Time Management; Persuasion; Active Learning.

Education/Training Programs: Broadcast Journalism; Business/Corporate Communications; Communication, Journalism, and Related Programs, Other; English Language and Literature, General; Family and Consumer Sciences/Human Sciences Communication; Journalism; Mass Communication/Media Studies; Publishing. **Related Knowledge/Courses:** Communications and Media; History and Archeology; Geography; Fine Arts; English Language; Clerical.

Education Administrators, Preschool and Child Care Center/Program

- Education/Training Required: Work experience plus degree
- Annual Earnings: $41,060
- Earnings Growth Potential: Medium
- Growth: 11.8%
- Annual Job Openings: 2,460
- Self-Employed: 4.2%

Hottest Fields (with Growth): Social Assistance, Except Child Day Care (20.4%); Advocacy, Grantmaking, and Civic Organizations (13.6%); Child Day Care Services (11.9%); Educational Services (9.6%); Health Care (8.5%).

Plan, direct, or coordinate the academic and nonacademic activities of preschool and child care centers or programs. Confer with parents and staff to discuss educational activities and policies and students' behavioral or learning problems. Prepare and maintain attendance, activity, planning, accounting, or personnel reports and records for officials and agencies or direct preparation and maintenance activities. Set educational standards and goals and help establish policies, procedures, and programs to carry them out. Monitor students' progress and provide students and teachers with assistance in resolving any problems. Determine allocations of funds for staff, supplies, materials, and equipment and authorize purchases. Recruit, hire, train, and evaluate primary and supplemental staff and recommend personnel actions for programs and services. Direct and coordinate activities of teachers or administrators at daycare centers, schools, public agencies, or institutions. Plan, direct, and monitor instructional methods and content of educational, vocational, or student activity programs. Review and interpret government codes and develop procedures to meet codes and to ensure facility safety, security, and maintenance. Determine the scope of educational program offerings and prepare drafts of program schedules and descriptions to estimate staffing and facility requirements. Review and evaluate new and current programs to determine their efficiency; effectiveness; and compliance with state, local, and federal regulations, and recommend any necessary modifications. Teach classes or courses or provide direct care to children. Prepare and submit budget requests or grant proposals to solicit program funding. Write articles, manuals, and other publications and assist in the distribution of promotional literature about programs and facilities.

Career Cluster: 05 Education and Training. **Pathway:** 05.1 Administration and Administrative Support.

Personality Type: Social-Enterprising-Conventional. **Skills:** Management of Financial Resources; Management of Personnel Resources; Management of Material Resources; Learning Strategies; Monitoring; Social Perceptiveness; Negotiation; Persuasion.

Education/Training Programs: Educational Administration and Supervision, Other; Educational Leadership and Administration, General; Educational, Instructional, and Curriculum Supervision; Elementary and Middle School Administration/Principalship. **Related Knowledge/Courses:** Personnel and Human Resources; Education and Training; Clerical; Philosophy and Theology; Therapy and Counseling; Sociology and Anthropology.

Electrical and Electronics Repairers, Commercial and Industrial Equipment

- Education/Training Required: Postsecondary vocational training
- Annual Earnings: $50,730
- Earnings Growth Potential: Medium
- Growth: 3.8%
- Annual Job Openings: 1,640
- Self-Employed: 0.0%

Hottest Fields (with Growth): Management, Scientific, and Technical Consulting Services (87.5%); Computer Systems Design and Related Services (45.8%); Construction (30.9%); Scientific Research and Development Services (27.5%); Employment Services (25.6%).

Repair, test, adjust, or install electronic equipment, such as industrial controls, transmitters, and antennas. Perform scheduled preventive maintenance tasks, such as checking, cleaning, and repairing equipment, to detect and prevent problems. Examine work orders and converse with equipment operators to detect equipment problems and to ascertain whether mechanical or human errors contributed to the problems. Operate equipment to demonstrate proper use and to analyze malfunctions. Set up and test industrial equipment to ensure that it functions properly. Test faulty equipment to diagnose malfunctions, using test equipment and software and applying knowledge of the functional operation of electronic units and systems. Repair and adjust equipment, machines, and defective components, replacing worn parts such as gaskets and seals in watertight electrical equipment. Calibrate testing instruments and installed or repaired equipment to prescribed specifications. Advise management regarding customer satisfaction, product performance, and suggestions for product improvements. Study blueprints, schematics, manuals, and other specifications to determine installation procedures. Inspect components of industrial equipment for accurate assembly and installation and for defects such as loose connections and frayed wires. Maintain equipment logs that record performance problems, repairs, calibrations, and tests. Coordinate efforts with other workers involved in installing and maintaining equipment or components. Maintain inventory of spare parts. Consult with customers, supervisors, and engineers to plan layout of equipment and to resolve problems in system operation and maintenance. Install repaired equipment in various settings, such as industrial or military establishments. Send defective units to the manufacturer or to a specialized repair shop for repair. Determine feasibility of using standardized equipment and develop specifications for equipment required to perform additional functions.

Career Cluster: 13 Manufacturing. **Pathway:** 13.3 Maintenance, Installation, and Repair.

Personality Type: Realistic-Investigative-Conventional. **Skills:** Installation; Repairing; Operation Monitoring; Troubleshooting; Equipment Maintenance; Operation and Control; Systems Analysis; Science.

Education/Training Programs: Computer Installation and Repair Technology/ Technician; Industrial Electronics Technology/Technician. **Related Knowledge/ Courses:** Mechanical; Computers and Electronics; Engineering and Technology; Design; Telecommunications; Physics.

Employment Interviewers

- Education/Training Required: Bachelor's degree
- Annual Earnings: $46,200
- Earnings Growth Potential: Medium
- Growth: 27.9%
- Annual Job Openings: 11,230
- Self-Employed: 1.6%

Our sources did not provide separate job openings data for this occupation. The job openings listed here are shared with Personnel Recruiters.

Hottest Fields (with Growth): Computer Systems Design and Related Services (54.4%); Management, Scientific, and Technical Consulting Services (46.9%); Software Publishers (42.3%); Scientific Research and Development Services (34.9%); Educational Services (33.9%).

Interview job applicants in employment office and refer them to prospective employers for consideration. Search application files, notify selected applicants of job openings, and refer qualified applicants to prospective employers. Contact employers to verify referral results. Record and evaluate various pertinent data. Inform applicants of job openings and details such as duties and responsibilities, compensation, benefits, schedules, working conditions, and promotion opportunities. Interview job applicants to match their qualifications with employers' needs, recording and evaluating applicant experience, education, training, and skills. Review employment applications and job orders to match applicants with job requirements, using manual or computerized file searches. Select qualified applicants or refer them to employers according to organization policy. Perform reference and background checks on applicants. Maintain records of applicants not selected for employment. Instruct job applicants in presenting a positive image by providing help with resume writing, personal appearance, and interview techniques. Refer applicants to services such as vocational counseling, literacy or language instruction, transportation assistance, vocational training, and child care. Contact employers to solicit orders for job vacancies, determining their requirements and recording relevant data such as job descriptions. Search for and recruit applicants for open positions through campus job fairs and advertisements. Provide background information on organizations with which interviews are scheduled. Conduct or arrange for skill, intelligence, or psychological testing of applicants and current employees. Hire workers and place them with employers needing temporary help.

Career Cluster: 04 Business, Management, and Administration. **Pathway:** 04.3 Human Resources.

Personality Type: Enterprising-Social-Conventional. **Skills:** Management of Personnel Resources; Service Orientation; Social Perceptiveness; Persuasion; Negotiation; Writing; Speaking; Instructing; Management of Financial Resources; Reading Comprehension.

Education/Training Programs: Human Resources Management/Personnel Administration, General; Labor and Industrial Relations. **Related Knowledge/ Courses:** Personnel and Human Resources; Sales and Marketing; Clerical; Therapy and Counseling; Customer and Personal Service; Administration and Management.

Employment, Recruitment, and Placement Specialists

See Employment Interviewers and Personnel Recruiters, described separately.

Environmental Compliance Inspectors

- Education/Training Required: Long-term on-the-job training
- Annual Earnings: $49,750
- Earnings Growth Potential: Medium
- Growth: 31.0%
- Annual Job Openings: 10,850
- Self-Employed: 1.4%

Our sources did not provide separate job openings data for this occupation. The job openings listed here are shared with Coroners; Equal Opportunity Representatives and Officers; Government Property Inspectors and Investigators; Licensing Examiners and Inspectors; and Regulatory Affairs Specialists.

Hottest Fields (with Growth): Management, Scientific, and Technical Consulting Services (120.9%); Computer Systems Design and Related Services (71.4%); Software Publishers (57.7%); Social Assistance, Except Child Day Care (54.6%); Scientific Research and Development Services (49.9%).

Inspect and investigate sources of pollution to protect the public and environment and ensure conformance with federal, state, and local regulations and ordinances. Determine the nature of code violations and actions to be taken and issue written notices of violation; participate in enforcement hearings as necessary. Examine permits, licenses, applications, and records to ensure compliance with licensing requirements. Prepare, organize, and maintain inspection records. Interview individuals to determine the nature of suspected violations and to obtain evidence of violations. Monitor follow-up actions in cases where violations were found and review compliance monitoring reports. Investigate complaints and suspected violations regarding illegal dumping, pollution, pesticides, product quality, or labeling laws. Inspect waste pretreatment, treatment, and disposal facilities and systems for conformance to federal, state, or local regulations. Inform individuals and groups of pollution control regulations and inspection findings and explain how problems can be corrected. Determine sampling locations and methods and collect water or wastewater samples for analysis, preserving samples with appropriate containers and preservation methods. Verify that hazardous chemicals are handled, stored, and disposed of in accordance with regulations. Research and keep informed of pertinent information and developments in areas such as EPA laws and regulations. Determine which sites and violation reports to investigate and coordinate compliance and enforcement activities with other government agencies. Observe and record field conditions, gathering, interpreting, and reporting data such as flow meter readings and chemical levels.

Career Cluster: 12 Law, Public Safety, Corrections, and Security. **Pathway:** 12.6 Inspection Services.

Personality Type: Conventional-Investigative-Realistic. **Skills:** Science; Negotiation; Writing; Reading Comprehension; Mathematics; Active Listening; Persuasion; Operation Monitoring.

Education/Training Program: Natural Resources Management and Policy, Other. **Related Knowledge/Courses:** Biology; Chemistry; Law and Government; Geography; Physics; Engineering and Technology.

Equal Opportunity Representatives and Officers

- Education/Training Required: Long-term on-the-job training
- Annual Earnings: $49,750
- Earnings Growth Potential: Medium
- Growth: 31.0%
- Annual Job Openings: 10,850
- Self-Employed: 1.4%

Our sources did not provide separate job openings data for this occupation. The job openings listed here are shared with Coroners; Environmental Compliance Inspectors; Government Property Inspectors and Investigators; Licensing Examiners and Inspectors; and Regulatory Affairs Specialists.

Hottest Fields (with Growth): Management, Scientific, and Technical Consulting Services (120.9%); Computer Systems Design and Related Services (71.4%); Software Publishers (57.7%); Social Assistance, Except Child Day Care (54.6%); Scientific Research and Development Services (49.9%).

Monitor and evaluate compliance with equal opportunity laws, guidelines, and policies to ensure that employment practices and contracting arrangements give equal opportunity without regard to race, religion, color, national origin, sex, age, or disability. Investigate employment practices and alleged violations of laws to document and correct discriminatory factors. Interpret civil rights laws and equal opportunity regulations for individuals and employers. Study equal opportunity complaints to clarify issues. Meet with persons involved in equal opportunity complaints to verify case information and to arbitrate and settle disputes. Coordinate, monitor, and revise complaint procedures to ensure timely processing and review of complaints. Prepare reports of selection, survey, and other statistics and recommendations for corrective action. Conduct surveys and evaluate findings to determine whether systematic discrimination exists. Develop guidelines for nondiscriminatory employment practices and monitor their implementation and impact. Review company contracts to determine actions required to meet governmental equal opportunity provisions. Counsel newly hired members of minority and disadvantaged groups, informing them about details of civil rights laws. Verify that all job descriptions are submitted for review and approval and that descriptions meet regulatory standards. Act as liaisons between minority placement agencies and employers or between job search committees and other equal opportunity administrators. Consult with community representatives to develop technical assistance agreements in accordance with governmental regulations.

Career Cluster: 12 Law, Public Safety, Corrections, and Security. **Pathway:** 12.6 Inspection Services.

Personality Type: Social-Enterprising-Conventional. **Skills:** Negotiation; Persuasion; Social Perceptiveness; Complex Problem Solving; Service Orientation; Judgment and Decision Making; Writing; Active Listening.

Education/Training Program: Public Administration and Social Service Professions, Other. **Related Knowledge/Courses:** Law and Government; Personnel and Human Resources; Clerical; English Language; Customer and Personal Service; Administration and Management.

Financial Analysts

- Education/Training Required: Bachelor's degree
- Annual Earnings: $73,670
- Earnings Growth Potential: Medium
- Growth: 19.8%
- Annual Job Openings: 9,520
- Self-Employed: 4.6%

Hottest Fields (with Growth): Management, Scientific, and Technical Consulting Services (104.1%); Computer Systems Design and Related Services (54.2%); Software Publishers (41.4%); Employment Services (36.5%); Scientific Research and Development Services (36.2%).

Conduct quantitative analyses of information affecting investment programs of public or private institutions. Assemble spreadsheets and draw charts and graphs used to illustrate technical reports, using computer. Analyze financial information to produce forecasts of business, industry, and economic conditions for use in making investment decisions. Maintain knowledge and stay abreast of developments in the fields of industrial technology, business, finance, and economic theory. Interpret data affecting investment programs, such as price, yield, stability, future trends in investment risks, and economic influences. Monitor fundamental economic, industrial, and corporate developments through the analysis of information obtained from financial publications and services, investment banking firms, government agencies, trade publications, company sources, and personal interviews. Recommend investments and investment timing to companies, investment firm staff, or the investing public. Determine the prices at which securities should be syndicated and offered to the public. Prepare plans of action for investment based on financial analyses. Present oral and written reports on general economic trends, individual corporations, and entire industries. Contact brokers and purchase investments for companies according to company policy. Collaborate with investment bankers to attract new corporate clients to securities firms.

Career Clusters: 04 Business, Management, and Administration; 06 Finance. **Pathways:** 04.2 Business, Financial Management, and Accounting; 06.1 Financial and Investment Planning.

Personality Type: Conventional-Investigative-Enterprising. **Skills:** Management of Financial Resources; Judgment and Decision Making; Mathematics; Systems Evaluation; Programming; Complex Problem Solving; Operations Analysis; Systems Analysis.

Education/Training Programs: Accounting and Business/Management; Accounting and Finance; Finance, General. **Related Knowledge/Courses:** No data available.

First-Line Supervisors/Managers of Personal Service Workers

- Education/Training Required: Work experience in a related occupation
- Annual Earnings: $35,330
- Earnings Growth Potential: Medium
- Growth: 15.4%
- Annual Job Openings: 9,080
- Self-Employed: 37.8%

Our sources did not provide separate job openings data for this occupation. The job openings listed here are shared with Spa Managers.

Hottest Fields (with Growth): Management, Scientific, and Technical Consulting Services (88.9%); Social Assistance, Except Child Day Care (51.0%); Employment Services (25.0%); Arts, Entertainment, and Recreation (24.7%); Educational Services (16.2%).

Supervise and coordinate activities of personal service workers such as flight attendants, hairdressers, or caddies. Requisition necessary supplies, equipment, and services. Inform workers about interests and special needs of specific groups. Participate in continuing education to stay abreast of industry trends and developments. Meet with managers and other supervisors to stay informed of changes affecting operations. Collaborate with staff members to plan and develop programs of events, schedules of activities, or menus. Train workers in proper operational procedures and functions, and explain company policies. Furnish customers with information on events and activities. Resolve customer complaints regarding worker performance and services rendered. Analyze and record personnel and operational data, and write related activity reports. Observe and evaluate workers' appearance and performance to ensure quality service and compliance with specifications. Inspect work areas and operating equipment to ensure conformance to established standards in areas such as cleanliness and maintenance. Assign work schedules, following work requirements, to ensure quality and timely delivery of service. Apply customer/guest feedback to service improvement efforts. Take disciplinary action to address performance problems. Recruit and hire staff members.

Career Cluster: 04 Business, Management, and Administration. **Pathway:** 04.1 Management.

Personality Type: Enterprising-Conventional-Social. **Skills:** Management of Personnel Resources; Social Perceptiveness; Service Orientation; Learning Strategies; Coordination; Writing; Judgment and Decision Making; Time Management.

Education/Training Program: Personal and Culinary Services, Other. **Related Knowledge/Courses:** Psychology; Therapy and Counseling; Education and Training; Philosophy and Theology; Public Safety and Security; Medicine and Dentistry.

General and Operations Managers

- Education/Training Required: Work experience plus degree
- Annual Earnings: $92,650
- Earnings Growth Potential: High
- Growth: −0.1%
- Annual Job Openings: 50,220
- Self-Employed: 0.9%

Hottest Fields (with Growth): Management, Scientific, and Technical Consulting Services (65.6%); Computer Systems Design and Related Services (28.7%); Social Assistance, Except Child Day Care (19.0%); Software Publishers (16.5%); Health Care (11.5%).

Plan, direct, or coordinate the operations of companies or public- and private-sector organizations. Duties and responsibilities include formulating policies, managing daily operations, and planning the use of materials and human resources, but are too diverse and general in nature to be classified in any one functional area of management or administration, such as personnel, purchasing, or administrative services. Includes owners and managers who head small business establishments whose duties are primarily managerial. Oversee activities directly related to making products or providing services. Direct and coordinate activities of businesses or departments concerned with the production, pricing, sales, or distribution of products. Review financial statements, sales and activity reports, and other performance data to measure productivity and goal achievement and to determine areas needing cost reduction and program improvement. Manage staff, preparing work schedules and assigning specific duties. Direct and coordinate organization's financial and budget activities to fund operations, maximize investments and increase efficiency. Establish and implement departmental policies, goals, objectives, and procedures, conferring with board members, organization officials, and staff members as necessary. Determine staffing requirements, and interview, hire, and train new employees, or oversee those personnel processes. Plan and direct activities such as sales promotions, coordinating with other department heads as required. Locate, select, and procure merchandise for resale, representing management in purchase negotiations. Perform sales floor work such as greeting and assisting customers, stocking shelves, and taking inventory. Manage the movement of goods into and out of production facilities. Recommend locations for new facilities or oversee the remodeling of current facilities. Plan store layouts and design displays.

Career Clusters: 04 Business, Management, and Administration; 07 Government and Public Administration. **Pathways:** 04.1 Management; 07.1 Governance.

Personality Type: Enterprising-Conventional-Social. **Skills:** Systems Analysis; Management of Material Resources; Management of Personnel Resources; Management of Financial Resources; Systems Evaluation; Negotiation; Operation Monitoring; Persuasion.

Education/Training Programs: Business Administration and Management, General; Entrepreneurship/Entrepreneurial Studies; International Business/Trade/Commerce; Public Administration. **Related Knowledge/Courses:** Economics and Accounting; Personnel and Human Resources; Administration and Management; Sales and Marketing; Clerical; Building and Construction.

Government Property Inspectors and Investigators

- Education/Training Required: Long-term on-the-job training
- Annual Earnings: $49,750
- Earnings Growth Potential: Medium
- Growth: 31.0%
- Annual Job Openings: 10,850
- Self-Employed: 1.4%

Our sources did not provide separate job openings data for this occupation. The job openings listed here are shared with Coroners; Environmental Compliance Inspectors; Equal Opportunity Representatives and Officers; Licensing Examiners and Inspectors; and Regulatory Affairs Specialists.

Hottest Fields (with Growth): Management, Scientific, and Technical Consulting Services (120.9%); Computer Systems Design and Related Services (71.4%); Software Publishers (57.7%); Social Assistance, Except Child Day Care (54.6%); Scientific Research and Development Services (49.9%).

Investigate or inspect government property to ensure compliance with contract agreements and government regulations. Prepare correspondence, reports of inspections or investigations, and recommendations for action. Inspect government-owned equipment and materials in the possession of private contractors to ensure compliance with contracts and regulations and to prevent misuse. Examine records, reports, and documents to establish facts and detect discrepancies. Inspect manufactured or processed products to ensure compliance with contract specifications and legal requirements. Locate and interview plaintiffs, witnesses, or representatives of business or government to gather facts relevant to inspections or alleged violations. Recommend legal or administrative action to protect government property. Submit samples of products to government laboratories for testing as required. Coordinate with and assist law enforcement agencies in matters of mutual concern. Testify in court or at administrative proceedings concerning findings of investigations. Collect, identify, evaluate, and preserve case evidence. Monitor investigations of suspected offenders to ensure that they are conducted in accordance with constitutional requirements. Investigate applications for special licenses or permits, as well as alleged violations of licenses or permits.

Career Cluster: 12 Law, Public Safety, Corrections, and Security. **Pathway:** 12.6 Inspection Services.

Personality Type: Conventional-Enterprising-Realistic. **Skills:** Quality Control Analysis; Technology Design; Science; Troubleshooting; Equipment Selection; Coordination; Operation and Control; Service Orientation.

Education/Training Program: Building/Home/Construction Inspection/ Inspector. **Related Knowledge/Courses:** Building and Construction; Engineering and Technology; Public Safety and Security; Mechanical; Transportation; Computers and Electronics.

Health Educators

- Education/Training Required: Bachelor's degree
- Annual Earnings: $44,340
- Earnings Growth Potential: High
- Growth: 18.2%
- Annual Job Openings: 2,600
- Self-Employed: 0.3%

Hottest Fields (with Growth): Management, Scientific, and Technical Consulting Services (91.5%); Employment Services (30.0%); Social Assistance, Except Child Day Care (25.9%); Educational Services (23.9%); Health Care (23.6%).

Promote, maintain, and improve individual and community health by assisting individuals and communities to adopt healthy behaviors. Collect and analyze data to identify community needs prior to planning, implementing, monitoring, and evaluating programs designed to encourage healthy lifestyles, policies, and environments. May also serve as a resource to assist individuals, other professionals, or the community and may administer fiscal resources for health education programs. Document activities, recording information such as the numbers of applications completed, presentations conducted, and persons assisted. Develop and present health education and promotion programs such as training workshops, conferences, and school or community presentations. Develop and maintain cooperative working relationships with agencies and organizations interested in public health care. Prepare and distribute health education materials, including reports; bulletins; and visual aids such as films, videotapes, photographs, and posters. Develop operational plans and policies necessary to achieve health education objectives and services. Collaborate with health specialists and civic groups to determine community health needs and the availability of services and to develop goals for meeting needs. Supervise professional and technical staff in implementing health programs, objectives, and goals. Design and conduct evaluations and diagnostic studies to assess the quality and performance of health education programs. Provide program information to the public by preparing and presenting press releases, conducting media campaigns, and/or maintaining program-related Web sites. Develop, prepare, and coordinate grant applications and grant-related activities to obtain funding for health education programs and related work. Provide guidance to agencies and organizations in the assessment of health education needs and in the development and delivery of health education programs.

Career Clusters: 08 Health Science; 10 Human Services. **Pathways:** 08.3 Health Informatics; 10.2 Counseling and Mental Health Services.

Personality Type: Social-Enterprising. **Skills:** Service Orientation; Social Perceptiveness; Monitoring; Learning Strategies; Speaking; Instructing; Coordination; Active Learning; Operations Analysis; Writing.

Education/Training Programs: Community Health Services/Liaison/Counseling; Health Communication; International Public Health/International Health; Maternal and Child Health; Public Health Education and Promotion. **Related Knowledge/Courses:** No data available.

Heating and Air Conditioning Mechanics and Installers

- Education/Training Required: Long-term on-the-job training
- Annual Earnings: $41,100
- Earnings Growth Potential: Medium
- Growth: 28.1%
- Annual Job Openings: 13,620
- Self-Employed: 15.5%

Our sources did not provide separate job openings data for this occupation. The job openings listed here are shared with Refrigeration Mechanics and Installers.

Hottest Fields (with Growth): Construction (43.0%); Computer Systems Design and Related Services (40.0%); Scientific Research and Development Services (19.2%); Employment Services (16.7%); Social Assistance, Except Child Day Care (13.3%).

Install, service, and repair heating and air conditioning systems in residences and commercial establishments. Obtain and maintain required certifications. Comply with all applicable standards, policies, and procedures, including safety procedures and the maintenance of a clean work area. Repair or replace defective equipment, components, or wiring. Test electrical circuits and components for continuity, using electrical test equipment. Reassemble and test equipment following repairs. Inspect and test system to verify system compliance with plans and specifications and to detect and locate malfunctions. Discuss heating-cooling system malfunctions with users to isolate problems or to verify that malfunctions have been corrected. Test pipe or tubing joints and connections for leaks, using pressure gauge or soap-and-water solution. Record and report all faults, deficiencies, and other unusual occurrences, as well as the time and materials expended on work orders. Adjust system controls to setting recommended by manufacturer to balance system, using hand tools. Recommend, develop, and perform preventive and general maintenance procedures such as cleaning, power-washing, and vacuuming equipment; oiling parts; and changing filters. Lay out and connect electrical wiring between controls and equipment according to wiring diagram, using electrician's hand tools. Install auxiliary components to heating-cooling equipment, such as expansion and discharge valves, air ducts, pipes, blowers, dampers, flues, and stokers, following blueprints. Assist with other work in coordination with repair and maintenance teams. Install, connect, and adjust thermostats, humidistats, and timers, using hand tools. Generate work orders that address deficiencies in need of correction. Join pipes or tubing to equipment and to fuel, water, or refrigerant source to form complete circuit. Assemble, position, and mount heating or cooling equipment, following blueprints.

Career Cluster: 02 Architecture and Construction. **Pathways:** 02.2 Construction; 02.3 Maintenance/Operations.

Personality Type: Realistic-Conventional-Investigative. **Skills:** Repairing; Installation; Equipment Maintenance; Troubleshooting; Systems Evaluation; Science; Systems Analysis; Coordination; Operation Monitoring.

Education/Training Programs: Heating, Air Conditioning, Ventilation and Refrigeration Maintenance Technology/Technician (HAC, HACR, HVAC, HVACR); Heating, Ventilation, Air Conditioning and Refrigeration Engineering Technology/Technician; Solar Energy Technology/Technician. **Related Knowledge/Courses:** Mechanical; Building and Construction; Design; Physics; Engineering and Technology; Sales and Marketing.

Heating, Air Conditioning, and Refrigeration Mechanics and Installers

See Heating and Air Conditioning Mechanics and Installers; and Refrigeration Mechanics and Installers, described separately.

Home Health Aides

- Education/Training Required: Short-term on-the-job training
- Annual Earnings: $20,480
- Earnings Growth Potential: Very low
- Growth: 50.0%
- Annual Job Openings: 55,270
- Self-Employed: 1.8%

Hottest Fields (with Growth): Social Assistance, Except Child Day Care (77.5%); Health Care (46.2%); Employment Services (24.4%); Child Day Care Services (11.8%); Educational Services (10.0%).

Provide routine, personal health care, such as bathing, dressing, or grooming, to elderly, convalescent, or disabled persons in the home of patients or in a residential care facility. Maintain records of patient care, condition, progress, or problems to report and discuss observations with supervisor or case manager. Provide patients with help moving in and out of beds, baths, wheelchairs, or automobiles and with dressing and grooming. Provide patients and families with emotional support and instruction in areas such as caring for infants, preparing healthy meals, living independently, or adapting to disability or illness. Change bed linens, wash and iron patients' laundry, and clean patients' quarters. Entertain, converse with, or read aloud to patients to keep them mentally healthy and alert. Plan, purchase, prepare, or serve meals to patients or other family members according to prescribed diets. Direct patients in simple prescribed exercises or in the use of braces or artificial limbs. Check patients' pulse, temperature, and respiration. Change dressings. Perform a variety of duties as requested by client, such as obtaining household supplies or running errands. Accompany clients to doctors' offices and on other trips outside the home, providing transportation, assistance, and companionship. Administer prescribed oral medications under written direction of physician or as directed by home care nurse and aide.

Career Cluster: 08 Health Science. **Pathway:** 08.1 Therapeutic Services.

Personality Type: Social-Realistic. **Skills:** None met the criteria.

Education/Training Program: Home Health Aide/Home Attendant Training. **Related Knowledge/Courses:** Medicine and Dentistry; Therapy and Counseling; Psychology.

Industrial Engineers

- Education/Training Required: Bachelor's degree
- Annual Earnings: $75,110
- Earnings Growth Potential: Low
- Growth: 14.2%
- Annual Job Openings: 8,540
- Self-Employed: 0.7%

Our sources did not provide separate job openings data for this occupation. The job openings listed here are shared with Human Factors Engineers and Ergonomists.

Hottest Fields (with Growth): Management, Scientific, and Technical Consulting Services (111.8%); Computer Systems Design and Related Services (64.5%); Software Publishers (47.4%); Scientific Research and Development Services (44.4%); Employment Services (40.1%).

Design, develop, test, and evaluate integrated systems for managing industrial production processes, including human work factors, quality control, inventory control, logistics and material flow, cost analysis, and production coordination. Analyze statistical data and product specifications to determine standards and establish quality and reliability objectives of finished product. Develop manufacturing methods, labor utilization standards, and cost analysis systems to promote efficient staff and facility utilization. Recommend methods for improving utilization of personnel, material, and utilities. Plan and establish sequence of operations to fabricate and assemble parts or products and to promote efficient utilization. Apply statistical methods and perform mathematical calculations to determine manufacturing processes, staff requirements, and production standards. Coordinate quality control objectives and activities to resolve production problems, maximize product reliability, and minimize cost. Confer with vendors, staff, and management personnel regarding purchases, procedures, product specifications, manufacturing capabilities, and project status. Draft and design layout of equipment, materials, and workspace to illustrate maximum efficiency, using drafting tools and computer. Communicate with management and user personnel to develop production and design standards. Estimate production cost and effect of product design changes for management review, action, and control. Formulate sampling procedures and designs and develop forms and instructions for recording, evaluating, and reporting quality and reliability data. Record or oversee recording of information to ensure currency of engineering drawings and documentation of production problems.

Career Cluster: 15 Science, Technology, Engineering, and Mathematics. **Pathway:** 15.1 Engineering and Technology.

Personality Type: Investigative-Conventional-Enterprising. **Skills:** Equipment Selection; Technology Design; Troubleshooting; Installation; Systems Analysis; Mathematics; Judgment and Decision Making; Negotiation.

Education/Training Program: Industrial Engineering. **Related Knowledge/ Courses:** No data available.

Industrial Machinery Mechanics

- Education/Training Required: Long-term on-the-job training
- Annual Earnings: $44,470
- Earnings Growth Potential: Low
- Growth: 7.3%
- Annual Job Openings: 6,240
- Self-Employed: 2.2%

Hottest Fields (with Growth): Management, Scientific, and Technical Consulting Services (118.2%); Scientific Research and Development Services (44.3%); Agriculture, Forestry, and Fishing (42.9%); Employment Services (39.8%); Construction (31.3%).

Repair, install, adjust, or maintain industrial production and processing machinery or refinery and pipeline distribution systems. Disassemble machinery and equipment to remove parts and make repairs. Repair and replace broken or malfunctioning components of machinery and equipment. Repair and maintain the operating condition of industrial production and processing machinery and equipment. Examine parts for defects such as breakage and excessive wear. Reassemble equipment after completion of inspections, testing, or repairs. Observe

123

and test the operation of machinery and equipment to diagnose malfunctions, using voltmeters and other testing devices. Operate newly repaired machinery and equipment to verify the adequacy of repairs. Clean, lubricate, and adjust parts, equipment, and machinery. Analyze test results, machine error messages, and information obtained from operators to diagnose equipment problems. Record repairs and maintenance performed. Study blueprints and manufacturers' manuals to determine correct installation and operation of machinery. Record parts and materials used, ordering or requisitioning new parts and materials as necessary. Cut and weld metal to repair broken metal parts, fabricate new parts, and assemble new equipment. Demonstrate equipment functions and features to machine operators.

Career Cluster: 13 Manufacturing. **Pathway:** 13.3 Maintenance, Installation, and Repair.

Personality Type: Realistic-Investigative-Conventional. **Skills:** Installation; Repairing; Equipment Maintenance; Operation Monitoring; Troubleshooting; Technology Design; Equipment Selection; Operation and Control.

Education/Training Programs: Heavy/Industrial Equipment Maintenance Technologies, Other; Industrial Mechanics and Maintenance Technology. **Related Knowledge/Courses:** Mechanical; Engineering and Technology; Building and Construction; Design; Chemistry; Physics.

Instructional Coordinators

- Education/Training Required: Master's degree
- Annual Earnings: $58,780
- Earnings Growth Potential: High
- Growth: 23.2%
- Annual Job Openings: 6,060
- Self-Employed: 2.9%

Our sources did not provide separate job openings data for this occupation. The job openings listed here are shared with Instructional Designers and Technologists.

Hottest Fields (with Growth): Management, Scientific, and Technical Consulting Services (88.7%); Computer Systems Design and Related Services (43.1%); Software Publishers (33.3%); Educational Services (27.6%); Employment Services (26.3%).

Develop instructional material, coordinate educational content, and incorporate current technology in specialized fields that provide guidelines to educators and instructors for developing curricula and conducting courses. Conduct or participate in workshops, committees, and conferences designed to promote the intellectual, social, and physical welfare of students. Plan and conduct teacher training programs and conferences dealing with new classroom procedures, instructional materials and equipment, and teaching aids. Advise teaching and administrative staff in curriculum development, use of materials and equipment, and implementation of state and federal programs and procedures. Recommend, order, or authorize purchase of instructional materials, supplies, equipment, and visual aids designed to meet student educational needs and district standards. Interpret and enforce provisions of state education codes and rules and regulations of state education boards. Confer with members of educational committees and advisory groups to obtain knowledge of subject areas and to relate curriculum materials to specific subjects, individual student needs, and occupational areas. Organize production and design of curriculum materials. Research, evaluate, and prepare recommendations on curricula, instructional methods, and materials for school systems. Observe work of teaching staff to evaluate performance and to recommend changes that could strengthen teaching skills. Develop instructional materials to be used by educators and instructors. Prepare grant proposals, budgets, and program policies and goals or assist in their preparation. Develop tests, questionnaires, and procedures that measure the effectiveness of curricula and use these tools to determine whether program objectives are being met. Update the content of educational programs to ensure that students are being trained with equipment and processes that are technologically current. Address public audiences to explain program objectives and to elicit support. Advise and teach students.

Career Cluster: 05 Education and Training. **Pathways:** 05.1 Administration and Administrative Support; 05.3 Teaching/Training.

Personality Type: Social-Investigative-Enterprising. **Skills:** Management of Financial Resources; Learning Strategies; Monitoring; Social Perceptiveness; Coordination; Time Management; Management of Personnel Resources; Persuasion.

Education/Training Programs: Curriculum and Instruction; Educational/Instructional Technology. **Related Knowledge/Courses:** Education and Training; Sociology and Anthropology; English Language; Personnel and Human Resources; Communications and Media; Psychology.

Kindergarten Teachers, Except Special Education

- Education/Training Required: Bachelor's degree
- Annual Earnings: $47,830
- Earnings Growth Potential: Low
- Growth: 15.0%
- Annual Job Openings: 6,300
- Self-Employed: 1.6%

Hottest Fields (with Growth): Social Assistance, Except Child Day Care (20.9%); Advocacy, Grantmaking, and Civic Organizations (18.2%); Educational Services (15.4%); Child Day Care Services (12.0%).

Teach elemental natural and social science, personal hygiene, music, art, and literature to children from 4 to 6 years of age. Promote physical, mental, and social development. May be required to hold state certification. Teach basic skills such as color, shape, number, and letter recognition; personal hygiene; and social skills. Establish and enforce rules for behavior and policies and procedures to maintain order among students. Observe and evaluate children's performance, behavior, social development, and physical health. Instruct students individually and in groups, adapting teaching methods to meet students' varying needs and interests. Read books to entire classes or to small groups. Demonstrate activities to children. Provide a variety of materials and resources for children to explore, manipulate, and use, both in learning activities and in imaginative play. Plan and conduct activities for a balanced program of instruction, demonstration, and work time that provides students with opportunities to observe, question, and investigate. Confer with parents or guardians, other teachers, counselors, and administrators to resolve students' behavioral and academic problems. Prepare children for later grades by encouraging them to explore learning opportunities and to persevere with challenging tasks. Establish clear objectives for all lessons, units, and projects and communicate those objectives to children. Prepare and implement remedial programs for students requiring extra help. Meet with parents and guardians to discuss their children's progress and to determine their priorities for their children and their resource needs. Prepare objectives and outlines for courses of study, following curriculum guidelines or requirements of states and schools. Organize and lead activities designed to promote physical, mental, and social development such as games, arts and crafts, music, and storytelling. Guide and counsel students with adjustment or academic problems or special academic interests. Identify children showing signs of emotional, developmental, or health-related problems and discuss them with supervisors, parents or guardians, and child development specialists.

Career Cluster: 05 Education and Training. **Pathway:** 05.3 Teaching/Training.

Personality Type: Social-Artistic. **Skills:** Learning Strategies; Instructing; Monitoring; Social Perceptiveness; Writing; Time Management; Coordination; Speaking.

Education/Training Program: Early Childhood Education and Teaching. **Related Knowledge/Courses:** History and Archeology; Geography; Sociology and Anthropology; Philosophy and Theology; Psychology; Education and Training.

Licensing Examiners and Inspectors
- Education/Training Required: Long-term on-the-job training
- Annual Earnings: $49,750
- Earnings Growth Potential: Medium
- Growth: 31.0%

- Annual Job Openings: 10,850
- Self-Employed: 1.4%

Our sources did not provide separate job openings data for this occupation. The job openings listed here are shared with Coroners; Environmental Compliance Inspectors; Equal Opportunity Representatives and Officers; Government Property Inspectors and Investigators; and Regulatory Affairs Specialists.

Hottest Fields (with Growth): Management, Scientific, and Technical Consulting Services (120.9%); Computer Systems Design and Related Services (71.4%); Software Publishers (57.7%); Social Assistance, Except Child Day Care (54.6%); Scientific Research and Development Services (49.9%).

Examine, evaluate, and investigate eligibility for, conformity with, or liability under licenses or permits. Issue licenses to individuals meeting standards. Evaluate applications, records, and documents in order to gather information about eligibility or liability issues. Administer oral, written, road, or flight tests to license applicants. Score tests and observe equipment operation and control in order to rate ability of applicants. Advise licensees and other individuals or groups concerning licensing, permit, or passport regulations. Warn violators of infractions or penalties. Prepare reports of activities, evaluations, recommendations, and decisions. Prepare correspondence to inform concerned parties of licensing decisions and of appeals processes.

Career Cluster: 12 Law, Public Safety, Corrections, and Security. **Pathway:** 12.6 Inspection Services.

Personality Type: Conventional-Enterprising. **Skills:** Speaking; Service Orientation; Judgment and Decision Making; Active Listening; Reading Comprehension.

Education/Training Program: Public Administration and Social Service Professions, Other. **Related Knowledge/Courses:** Clerical; Customer and Personal Service; Law and Government; Foreign Language; Psychology; Public Safety and Security.

Loan Counselors

- Education/Training Required: Bachelor's degree
- Annual Earnings: $37,320
- Earnings Growth Potential: Low
- Growth: 16.3%
- Annual Job Openings: 880
- Self-Employed: 3.4%

Hottest Fields (with Growth): Management, Scientific, and Technical Consulting Services (84.0%); Employment Services (40.0%); Educational Services (39.4%); Health Care (19.1%); Social Assistance, Except Child Day Care (18.1%).

127

Provide guidance to prospective loan applicants who have problems qualifying for traditional loans. Guidance may include determining the best type of loan and explaining loan requirements or restrictions. Check loan agreements to ensure that they are complete and accurate according to policies. Refer loans to loan committees for approval. Approve loans within specified limits. Submit applications to credit analysts for verification and recommendation. Analyze applicants' financial status, credit, and property evaluations to determine feasibility of granting loans. Interview applicants and request specified information for loan applications. Establish payment priorities according to credit terms and interest rates in order to reduce clients' overall costs. Contact applicants or creditors to resolve questions about applications or to assist with completion of paperwork. Maintain current knowledge of credit regulations. Calculate amount of debt and funds available in order to plan methods of payoff and to estimate time for debt liquidation. Analyze potential loan markets to find opportunities to promote loans and financial services. Review billing for accuracy. Supervise loan personnel. Maintain and review account records, updating and recategorizing them according to status changes. Assist in selection of financial award candidates, using electronic databases to certify loan eligibility. Confer with underwriters to resolve mortgage application problems. Inform individuals and groups about the financial assistance available to college or university students. Match students' needs and eligibility with available financial aid programs in order to provide informed recommendations. Contact creditors to explain clients' financial situations and to arrange for payment adjustments so that payments are feasible for clients and agreeable to creditors. Petition courts to transfer titles and deeds of collateral to banks. Contact borrowers with delinquent accounts to obtain payment in full or to negotiate repayment plans.

Career Cluster: 06 Finance. **Pathways:** 06.1 Financial and Investment Planning; 06.3 Banking and Related Services.

Personality Type: Enterprising-Social-Conventional. **Skills:** Service Orientation; Active Listening; Speaking; Persuasion; Coordination; Instructing; Reading Comprehension; Mathematics.

Education/Training Programs: Banking and Financial Support Services; Finance and Financial Management Services, Other. **Related Knowledge/Courses:** No data available.

Maintenance and Repair Workers, General

- Education/Training Required: Moderate-term on-the-job training
- Annual Earnings: $34,620
- Earnings Growth Potential: Medium
- Growth: 10.9%
- Annual Job Openings: 35,750
- Self-Employed: 1.1%

Hottest Fields (with Growth): Management, Scientific, and Technical Consulting Services (91.5%); Computer Systems Design and Related Services (44.8%); Software Publishers (33.3%); Scientific Research and Development Services (28.9%); Employment Services (28.0%).

Perform work involving the skills of two or more maintenance or craft occupations to keep machines, mechanical equipment, or the structure of an establishment in repair. Duties may involve pipe fitting; boiler making; insulating; welding; machining; carpentry; repairing electrical or mechanical equipment; installing, aligning, and balancing new equipment; and repairing buildings, floors, or stairs. Repair or replace defective equipment parts, using hand tools and power tools, and reassemble equipment. Perform routine preventive maintenance to ensure that machines continue to run smoothly, building systems operate efficiently, and the physical condition of buildings does not deteriorate. Inspect drives, motors, and belts; check fluid levels; replace filters; and perform other maintenance actions, following checklists. Use tools ranging from common hand and power tools, such as hammers, hoists, saws, drills, and wrenches, to precision measuring instruments and electrical and electronic testing devices. Assemble, install, or repair wiring, electrical and electronic components, pipe systems and plumbing, machinery, and equipment. Diagnose mechanical problems and determine how to correct them, checking blueprints, repair manuals, and parts catalogs as necessary. Inspect, operate, and test machinery and equipment to diagnose machine malfunctions. Record maintenance and repair work performed and the costs of the work. Clean and lubricate shafts, bearings, gears, and other parts of machinery. Dismantle devices to gain access to and remove defective parts, using hoists, cranes, hand tools, and power tools. Plan and lay out repair work, using diagrams, drawings, blueprints, maintenance manuals, and schematic diagrams. Adjust functional parts of devices and control instruments, using hand tools, levels, plumb bobs, and straightedges. Order parts, supplies, and equipment from catalogs and suppliers or obtain them from storerooms. Paint and repair roofs, windows, doors, floors, woodwork, plaster, drywall, and other parts of building structures.

Career Cluster: 02 Architecture and Construction. **Pathway:** 02.2 Construction.

Personality Type: Realistic-Conventional-Investigative. **Skills:** Equipment Maintenance; Installation; Repairing; Troubleshooting; Operation Monitoring; Operation and Control; Equipment Selection; Technology Design; Quality Control Analysis.

Education/Training Program: Building/Construction Site Management/Manager. **Related Knowledge/Courses:** Building and Construction; Mechanical; Design; Physics; Engineering and Technology; Public Safety and Security.

Market Research Analysts

- Education/Training Required: Bachelor's degree
- Annual Earnings: $61,580
- Earnings Growth Potential: High
- Growth: 28.1%
- Annual Job Openings: 13,730
- Self-Employed: 6.8%

Hottest Fields (with Growth): Management, Scientific, and Technical Consulting Services (84.0%); Employment Services (46.1%); Computer Systems Design and Related Services (43.1%); Software Publishers (41.2%); Advertising and Public Relations Services (40.9%).

Research market conditions in local, regional, or national areas to determine potential sales of a product or service. May gather information on competitors, prices, sales, and methods of marketing and distribution. May use survey results to create a marketing campaign based on regional preferences and buying habits. Collect and analyze data on customer demographics, preferences, needs, and buying habits to identify potential markets and factors affecting product demand. Prepare reports of findings, illustrating data graphically and translating complex findings into written text. Measure and assess customer and employee satisfaction. Forecast and track marketing and sales trends, analyzing collected data. Seek and provide information to help companies determine their position in the marketplace. Measure the effectiveness of marketing, advertising, and communications programs and strategies. Conduct research on consumer opinions and marketing strategies, collaborating with marketing professionals, statisticians, pollsters, and other professionals. Attend staff conferences to provide management with information and proposals concerning the promotion, distribution, design, and pricing of company products or services. Gather data on competitors and analyze their prices, sales, and method of marketing and distribution. Monitor industry statistics and follow trends in trade literature. Devise and evaluate methods and procedures for collecting data, such as surveys, opinion polls, or questionnaires, or arrange to obtain existing data.

Career Clusters: 04 Business, Management, and Administration; 14 Marketing, Sales, and Service; 15 Science, Technology, Engineering, and Mathematics. **Pathways:** 04.1 Management; 14.5 Marketing Information Management and Research; 15.3 Science and Mathematics.

Personality Type: Investigative-Enterprising-Conventional. **Skills:** Writing; Negotiation; Persuasion; Judgment and Decision Making; Reading Comprehension; Management of Financial Resources; Coordination; Active Listening; Time Management; Operations Analysis.

Education/Training Programs: Applied Economics; Business/Managerial Economics; Econometrics and Quantitative Economics; Economics, General;

International Economics; Marketing Research. **Related Knowledge/Courses:** No data available.

Mechanical Engineers

- Education/Training Required: Bachelor's degree
- Annual Earnings: $77,020
- Earnings Growth Potential: Low
- Growth: 6.0%
- Annual Job Openings: 7,570
- Self-Employed: 2.3%

Our sources did not provide separate job openings data for this occupation. The job openings listed here are shared with Automotive Engineers and Fuel Cell Engineers.

Hottest Fields (with Growth): Management, Scientific, and Technical Consulting Services (92.7%); Computer Systems Design and Related Services (50.5%); Software Publishers (38.5%); Construction (31.2%); Advocacy, Grantmaking, and Civic Organizations (23.8%).

Perform engineering duties in planning and designing tools, engines, machines, and other mechanically functioning equipment. Oversee installation, operation, maintenance, and repair of such equipment as centralized heat, gas, water, and steam systems. Read and interpret blueprints, technical drawings, schematics, and computer-generated reports. Confer with engineers and other personnel to implement operating procedures, resolve system malfunctions, and provide technical information. Research and analyze customer design proposals, specifications, manuals, and other data to evaluate the feasibility, cost, and maintenance requirements of designs or applications. Specify system components or direct modification of products to ensure conformance with engineering design and performance specifications. Research, design, evaluate, install, operate, and maintain mechanical products, equipment, systems, and processes to meet requirements, applying knowledge of engineering principles. Investigate equipment failures and difficulties to diagnose faulty operation and to make recommendations to maintenance crew. Oversee installation, operation, maintenance, and repair to ensure that machines and equipment are installed and functioning according to specifications. Conduct research that tests and analyzes the feasibility, design, operation, and performance of equipment, components, and systems. Recommend design modifications to eliminate machine or system malfunctions. Develop, coordinate, and monitor all aspects of production, including selection of manufacturing methods, fabrication, and operation of product designs. Estimate costs and submit bids for engineering, construction, or extraction projects and prepare contract documents.

Career Cluster: 15 Science, Technology, Engineering, and Mathematics. **Pathway:** 15.1 Engineering and Technology.

Personality Type: Investigative-Realistic-Conventional. **Skills:** Science; Operations Analysis; Installation; Complex Problem Solving; Mathematics; Systems Analysis; Judgment and Decision Making; Coordination.

Education/Training Program: Mechanical Engineering. **Related Knowledge/ Courses:** No data available.

Medical and Public Health Social Workers

- Education/Training Required: Bachelor's degree
- Annual Earnings: $46,300
- Earnings Growth Potential: Medium
- Growth: 22.4%
- Annual Job Openings: 6,590
- Self-Employed: 2.2%

Hottest Fields (with Growth): Management, Scientific, and Technical Consulting Services (92.9%); Social Assistance, Except Child Day Care (58.0%); Scientific Research and Development Services (30.8%); Employment Services (25.3%); Health Care (23.0%).

Provide persons, families, or vulnerable populations with the psychosocial support needed to cope with chronic, acute, or terminal illnesses such as Alzheimer's, cancer, or AIDS. Services include advising family caregivers, providing patient education and counseling, and making necessary referrals for other social services. Advocate for clients or patients to resolve crises. Collaborate with other professionals to evaluate patients' medical or physical condition and to assess client needs. Refer patients, clients, or families to community resources to assist in recovery from mental or physical illnesses and to provide access to services such as financial assistance, legal aid, housing, job placement, or education. Counsel clients and patients in individual and group sessions to help them overcome dependencies, recover from illnesses, and adjust to life. Use consultation data and social work experience to plan and coordinate client or patient care and rehabilitation, following through to ensure service efficacy. Plan discharge from care facility to home or other care facility. Organize support groups or counsel family members to assist them in understanding, dealing with, and supporting clients or patients. Modify treatment plans to comply with changes in clients' statuses. Monitor, evaluate, and record client progress according to measurable goals described in treatment and care plans. Identify environmental impediments to client or patient progress through interviews and review of patient records. Supervise and direct other workers providing services to clients or patients. Develop or advise on social policy and assist in community development. Investigate child abuse or neglect cases and take authorized protective action when necessary. Oversee Medicaid- and Medicare-related paperwork and recordkeeping in hospitals.

Career Cluster: 10 Human Services. **Pathway:** 10.2 Counseling and Mental Health Services.

Personality Type: Social-Investigative. **Skills:** Social Perceptiveness; Service Orientation; Systems Analysis; Systems Evaluation; Management of Personnel Resources; Writing; Persuasion; Negotiation.

Education/Training Program: Clinical/Medical Social Work. **Related Knowledge/Courses:** No data available.

Medical Assistants

- Education/Training Required: Moderate-term on-the-job training
- Annual Earnings: $28,650
- Earnings Growth Potential: Low
- Growth: 33.9%
- Annual Job Openings: 21,780
- Self-Employed: 0.0%

Hottest Fields (with Growth): Management, Scientific, and Technical Consulting Services (83.9%); Health Care (35.3%); Scientific Research and Development Services (25.9%); Social Assistance, Except Child Day Care (24.6%); Employment Services (21.6%).

Perform administrative and certain clinical duties under the direction of physicians. Administrative duties may include scheduling appointments, maintaining medical records, billing, and coding for insurance purposes. Clinical duties may include taking and recording vital signs and medical histories, preparing patients for examination, drawing blood, and administering medications as directed by physician. Record patients' medical history, vital statistics, and information such as test results in medical records. Prepare treatment rooms for patient examinations, keeping the rooms neat and clean. Interview patients to obtain medical information and measure their vital signs, weights, and heights. Authorize drug refills and provide prescription information to pharmacies. Clean and sterilize instruments and dispose of contaminated supplies. Prepare and administer medications as directed by a physician. Show patients to examination rooms and prepare them for the physician. Explain treatment procedures, medications, diets, and physicians' instructions to patients. Help physicians examine and treat patients, handing them instruments and materials or performing such tasks as giving injections or removing sutures. Collect blood, tissue, or other laboratory specimens, log the specimens, and prepare them for testing. Perform routine laboratory tests and sample analyses. Contact medical facilities or departments to schedule patients for tests or admission. Operate X-ray, electrocardiogram (EKG), and other equipment to administer routine diagnostic tests. Change dressings on wounds. Set up medical laboratory equipment. Perform general office duties such as answering telephones, taking dictation, or completing insurance forms.

Career Cluster: 08 Health Science. **Pathways:** 08.2 Diagnostics Services; 08.3 Health Informatics.

Personality Type: Social-Conventional-Realistic. **Skills:** Systems Analysis; Operation Monitoring.

Education/Training Programs: Allied Health and Medical Assisting Services, Other; Anesthesiologist Assistant Training; Chiropractic Assistant/Technician Training; Medical Administrative/Executive Assistant and Medical Secretary Training; Medical Insurance Coding Specialist/Coder; Medical Office Assistant/Specialist Training; Medical Office Management/Administration; Medical Reception/Receptionist; Medical/Clinical Assistant Training; Ophthalmic Technician/Technologist Training; Optometric Technician/Assistant Training; others. **Related Knowledge/Courses:** Medicine and Dentistry; Clerical; Psychology; Therapy and Counseling; Customer and Personal Service; Public Safety and Security.

Medical Scientists, Except Epidemiologists

- Education/Training Required: Doctoral degree
- Annual Earnings: $74,590
- Earnings Growth Potential: High
- Growth: 40.4%
- Annual Job Openings: 6,620
- Self-Employed: 2.5%

Hottest Fields (with Growth): Management, Scientific, and Technical Consulting Services (122.2%); Computer Systems Design and Related Services (62.5%); Scientific Research and Development Services (50.0%); Employment Services (48.5%); Health Care (45.5%).

Conduct research dealing with the understanding of human diseases and the improvement of human health. Engage in clinical investigation or other research, production, technical writing, or related activities. Conduct research to develop methodologies, instrumentation, and procedures for medical application, analyzing data and presenting findings. Plan and direct studies to investigate human or animal disease, preventive methods, and treatments for disease. Follow strict safety procedures when handling toxic materials to avoid contamination. Evaluate effects of drugs, gases, pesticides, parasites, and microorganisms at various levels. Teach principles of medicine and medical and laboratory procedures to physicians, residents, students, and technicians. Prepare and analyze organ, tissue, and cell samples to identify toxicity, bacteria, or microorganisms or to study cell structure. Standardize drug dosages, methods of immunization, and procedures for manufacture of drugs and medicinal compounds. Investigate cause, progress, life cycle, or mode of transmission of diseases or parasites. Confer with health department, industry personnel, physicians, and others to develop health safety standards and public health improvement programs. Study animal and human health and physiological processes.

Career Clusters: 08 Health Science; 15 Science, Technology, Engineering, and Mathematics. **Pathways:** 08.1 Therapeutic Services; 15.3 Science and Mathematics.

Personality Type: Investigative-Realistic-Artistic. **Skills:** Science; Management of Financial Resources; Judgment and Decision Making; Reading Comprehension; Writing; Time Management; Complex Problem Solving; Active Listening; Instructing.

Education/Training Programs: Anatomy; Biochemistry; Biomedical Sciences, General; Biophysics; Biostatistics; Cardiovascular Science; Cell Physiology; Cell/Cellular Biology and Histology; Endocrinology; Environmental Toxicology; Epidemiology; Exercise Physiology; Human/Medical Genetics; Immunology; Medical Microbiology and Bacteriology; Medical Scientist; Molecular Biology; Molecular Pharmacology; Molecular Physiology; Molecular Toxicology; Neuropharmacology; Oncology and Cancer Biology; Pathology/Experimental Pathology; others. **Related Knowledge/Courses:** No data available.

Network and Computer Systems Administrators

- Education/Training Required: Bachelor's degree
- Annual Earnings: $67,710
- Earnings Growth Potential: Medium
- Growth: 23.2%
- Annual Job Openings: 13,550
- Self-Employed: 0.8%

Our sources did not provide separate job openings data for this occupation. The job openings listed here are shared with Computer Security Specialists.

Hottest Fields (with Growth): Management, Scientific, and Technical Consulting Services (83.8%); Computer Systems Design and Related Services (71.7%); Software Publishers (55.2%); Health Care (41.1%); Social Assistance, Except Child Day Care (29.7%).

Install, configure, and support organizations' local area networks (LANs), wide area networks (WANs), and Internet systems or segments of network systems. Maintain network hardware and software. Monitor networks to ensure network availability to all system users and perform necessary maintenance to support network availability. May supervise other network support and client server specialists and plan, coordinate, and implement network security measures. Maintain and administer computer networks and related computing environments, including computer hardware, systems software, applications software, and all configurations. Perform data backups and disaster recovery operations.

135

Diagnose, troubleshoot, and resolve hardware, software, or other network and system problems and replace defective components when necessary. Plan, coordinate, and implement network security measures to protect data, software, and hardware. Configure, monitor, and maintain e-mail applications or virus protection software. Operate master consoles to monitor the performance of computer systems and networks and to coordinate computer network access and use. Design, configure, and test computer hardware, networking software, and operating system software. Monitor network performance to determine whether adjustments need to be made and to determine where changes will need to be made in the future. Confer with network users about how to solve existing system problems. Research new technologies by attending seminars, reading trade articles, or taking classes and implement or recommend the implementation of new technologies. Analyze equipment performance records to determine the need for repair or replacement.

Career Cluster: 11 Information Technology. **Pathways:** 11.1 Network Systems; 11.2 Information Support Services; 11.4 Programming and Software Development.

Personality Type: Investigative-Realistic-Conventional. **Skills:** Programming; Systems Evaluation; Systems Analysis; Operation Monitoring; Repairing; Quality Control Analysis; Troubleshooting; Equipment Maintenance; Technology Design.

Education/Training Programs: Computer and Information Sciences and Support Services, Other; Computer and Information Sciences, General; Computer and Information Systems Security/Information Assurance; Computer Systems Analysis/Analyst; Computer Systems Networking and Telecommunications; Information Science/Studies; Network and System Administration/Administrator; System, Networking, and LAN/WAN Management/Manager. **Related Knowledge/Courses:** No data available.

Network Systems and Data Communications Analysts

- Education/Training Required: Bachelor's degree
- Annual Earnings: $73,250
- Earnings Growth Potential: High
- Growth: 53.4%
- Annual Job Openings: 20,830
- Self-Employed: 19.4%

Our sources did not provide separate job openings data for this occupation. The job openings listed here are shared with Telecommunications Specialists.

Hottest Fields (with Growth): Management, Scientific, and Technical Consulting Services (148.2%); Computer Systems Design and Related Services (95.6%);

Software Publishers (75.7%); Social Assistance, Except Child Day Care (68.7%); Scientific Research and Development Services (67.4%).

Analyze, design, test, and evaluate network systems, such as local area networks (LAN); wide area networks (WAN); and Internet, intranet, and other data communications systems. Perform network modeling, analysis, and planning. Research and recommend network and data communications hardware and software. Includes telecommunications specialists who deal with the interfacing of computer and communications equipment. May supervise computer programmers. Maintain needed files by adding and deleting files on the network server and backing up files to guarantee their safety in the event of problems with the network. Monitor system performance and provide security measures, troubleshooting, and maintenance as needed. Assist users to diagnose and solve data communication problems. Set up user accounts, regulating and monitoring file access to ensure confidentiality and proper use. Design and implement systems, network configurations, and network architecture, including hardware and software technology, site locations, and integration of technologies. Maintain the peripherals, such as printers, that are connected to the network. Identify areas of operation that need upgraded equipment such as modems, fiber-optic cables, and telephone wires. Train users in use of equipment. Develop and write procedures for installation, use, and troubleshooting of communications hardware and software. Adapt and modify existing software to meet specific needs. Work with other engineers, systems analysts, programmers, technicians, scientists, and top-level managers in the design, testing, and evaluation of systems. Test and evaluate hardware and software to determine efficiency, reliability, and compatibility with existing system and make purchase recommendations.

Career Cluster: 11 Information Technology. **Pathways:** 11.1 Network Systems; 11.2 Information Support Services; 11.4 Programming and Software Development.

Personality Type: Investigative-Conventional. **Skills:** Installation; Technology Design; Troubleshooting; Systems Analysis; Programming; Systems Evaluation; Management of Material Resources; Operations Analysis.

Education/Training Programs: Computer and Information Sciences, General; Computer and Information Systems Security/Information Assurance; Computer Systems Analysis/Analyst; Computer Systems Networking and Telecommunications; Information Technology. **Related Knowledge/Courses:** No data available.

Occupational Therapists

- Education/Training Required: Master's degree
- Annual Earnings: $69,630
- Earnings Growth Potential: Low

- Growth: 25.6%
- Annual Job Openings: 4,580
- Self-Employed: 7.0%

Our sources did not provide separate job openings data for this occupation. The job openings listed here are shared with Low Vision Therapists, Orientation and Mobility Specialists, and Vision Rehabilitation Therapists.

Hottest Fields (with Growth): Social Assistance, Except Child Day Care (46.0%); Health Care (37.1%); Employment Services (20.9%); Child Day Care Services (11.8%); Educational Services (10.3%).

Assess, plan, organize, and participate in rehabilitative programs that help restore vocational, homemaking, and daily living skills, as well as general independence, to disabled persons. Plan, organize, and conduct occupational therapy programs in hospital, institutional, or community settings to help rehabilitate those impaired because of illness, injury, or psychological or developmental problems. Test and evaluate patients' physical and mental abilities and analyze medical data to determine realistic rehabilitation goals for patients. Select activities that will help individuals learn work and life-management skills within limits of their mental and physical capabilities. Evaluate patients' progress and prepare reports that detail progress. Complete and maintain necessary records. Train caregivers to provide for the needs of patients during and after therapies. Recommend changes in patients' work or living environments, consistent with their needs and capabilities. Develop and participate in health promotion programs, group activities, or discussions to promote client health, facilitate social adjustment, alleviate stress, and prevent physical or mental disability. Consult with rehabilitation team to select activity programs and coordinate occupational therapy with other therapeutic activities. Plan and implement programs and social activities to help patients learn work and school skills and adjust to handicaps. Design and create, or requisition, special supplies and equipment such as splints, braces and computer-aided adaptive equipment. Conduct research in occupational therapy.

Career Cluster: 08 Health Science. **Pathway:** 08.1 Therapeutic Services.

Personality Type: Social-Investigative. **Skills:** Service Orientation; Systems Evaluation; Management of Personnel Resources; Systems Analysis; Negotiation.

Education/Training Program: Occupational Therapy/Therapist. **Related Knowledge/Courses:** Therapy and Counseling; Psychology; Sociology and Anthropology; Medicine and Dentistry; Biology; Education and Training.

Office Clerks, General

- Education/Training Required: Short-term on-the-job training
- Annual Earnings: $26,140
- Earnings Growth Potential: Medium

- Growth: 11.9%
- Annual Job Openings: 77,090
- Self-Employed: 0.4%

Hottest Fields (with Growth): Management, Scientific, and Technical Consulting Services (65.6%); Computer Systems Design and Related Services (40.3%); Software Publishers (28.6%); Health Care (27.0%); Social Assistance, Except Child Day Care (23.2%).

Perform duties too varied and diverse to be classified in any specific office clerical occupation requiring limited knowledge of office management systems and procedures. Clerical duties may be assigned in accordance with the office procedures of individual establishments and may include a combination of answering telephones, bookkeeping, typing or word processing, stenography, office machine operation, and filing. Collect, count, and disburse money; do basic bookkeeping; and complete banking transactions. Communicate with customers, employees, and other individuals to answer questions, disseminate or explain information, take orders, and address complaints. Answer telephones, direct calls, and take messages. Compile, copy, sort, and file records of office activities, business transactions, and other activities. Complete and mail bills, contracts, policies, invoices, or checks. Operate office machines such as photocopiers and scanners, facsimile machines, voice mail systems, and personal computers. Compute, record, and proofread data and other information, such as records or reports. Maintain and update filing, inventory, mailing, and database systems, either manually or using a computer. Open, sort, and route incoming mail; answer correspondence; and prepare outgoing mail. Review files, records, and other documents to obtain information to respond to requests. Deliver messages and run errands. Inventory and order materials, supplies, and services. Complete work schedules, manage calendars, and arrange appointments. Process and prepare documents such as business or government forms and expense reports. Monitor and direct the work of lower-level clerks. Type, format, proofread, and edit correspondence and other documents from notes or dictating machines, using computers or typewriters.

Career Cluster: 04 Business, Management, and Administration. **Pathway:** 04.6 Administrative and Information Support.

Personality Type: Conventional-Enterprising-Realistic. **Skills:** None met the criteria.

Education/Training Program: General Office Occupations and Clerical Services. **Related Knowledge/Courses:** Clerical; Economics and Accounting; Customer and Personal Service; Personnel and Human Resources; Mathematics; Computers and Electronics.

Optometrists

- Education/Training Required: First professional degree
- Annual Earnings: $96,140
- Earnings Growth Potential: High
- Growth: 24.4%
- Annual Job Openings: 2,010
- Self-Employed: 24.6%

Hottest Fields (with Growth): Health Care (35.4%); Advocacy, Grantmaking, and Civic Organizations (14.3%); Educational Services (14.3%); Clothing, Accessory, and General Merchandise Stores (3.0%).

Diagnose, manage, and treat conditions and diseases of the human eye and visual system. Examine eyes and visual systems, diagnose problems or impairments, prescribe corrective lenses, and provide treatment. May prescribe therapeutic drugs to treat specific eye conditions. Examine eyes, using observation, instruments, and pharmaceutical agents, to determine visual acuity and perception, focus, and coordination and to diagnose diseases and other abnormalities such as glaucoma or color blindness. Prescribe medications to treat eye diseases if state laws permit. Analyze test results and develop treatment plans. Prescribe, supply, fit, and adjust eyeglasses, contact lenses, and other vision aids. Educate and counsel patients on contact lens care, visual hygiene, lighting arrangements, and safety factors. Remove foreign bodies from eyes. Consult with and refer patients to ophthalmologist or other health care practitioners if additional medical treatment is determined necessary. Provide patients undergoing eye surgeries such as cataract and laser vision correction, with pre- and post-operative care. Prescribe therapeutic procedures to correct or conserve vision.

Career Cluster: 08 Health Science. **Pathway:** 08.1 Therapeutic Services.

Personality Type: Investigative-Social-Realistic. **Skills:** Reading Comprehension; Quality Control Analysis; Systems Analysis; Systems Evaluation; Judgment and Decision Making; Service Orientation; Operation and Control.

Education/Training Program: Optometry (OD). **Related Knowledge/Courses:** Medicine and Dentistry; Biology; Therapy and Counseling; Physics; Sales and Marketing; Economics and Accounting.

Personnel Recruiters

- Education/Training Required: Bachelor's degree
- Annual Earnings: $46,200
- Earnings Growth Potential: Medium
- Growth: 27.9%
- Annual Job Openings: 11,230
- Self-Employed: 1.6%

Our sources did not provide separate job openings data for this occupation. The job openings listed here are shared with Employment Interviewers.

Hottest Fields (with Growth): Computer Systems Design and Related Services (54.4%); Management, Scientific, and Technical Consulting Services (46.9%); Software Publishers (42.3%); Scientific Research and Development Services (34.9%); Educational Services (33.9%).

Seek out, interview, and screen applicants to fill existing and future job openings and promote career opportunities within an organization. Establish and maintain relationships with hiring managers to stay abreast of current and future hiring and business needs. Interview applicants to obtain information on work history, training, education, and job skills. Maintain current knowledge of Equal Employment Opportunity (EEO) and affirmative action guidelines and laws, such as the Americans with Disabilities Act (ADA). Perform searches for qualified candidates according to relevant job criteria, using computer databases, networking, Internet recruiting resources, cold calls, media, recruiting firms, and employee referrals. Prepare and maintain employment records. Contact applicants to inform them of employment possibilities, consideration, and selection. Inform potential applicants about facilities, operations, benefits, and job or career opportunities in organizations. Screen and refer applicants to hiring personnel in the organization, making hiring recommendations when appropriate. Arrange for interviews and provide travel arrangements as necessary. Advise managers and employees on staffing policies and procedures. Review and evaluate applicant qualifications or eligibility for specified licensing according to established guidelines and designated licensing codes. Hire applicants and authorize paperwork assigning them to positions. Conduct reference and background checks on applicants. Evaluate recruitment and selection criteria to ensure conformance to professional, statistical, and testing standards, recommending revision as needed. Recruit applicants for open positions, arranging job fairs with college campus representatives. Advise management on organizing, preparing, and implementing recruiting and retention programs.

Career Cluster: 04 Business, Management, and Administration. **Pathway:** 04.3 Human Resources.

Personality Type: Enterprising-Social-Conventional. **Skills:** Management of Personnel Resources; Negotiation; Persuasion; Management of Financial Resources; Service Orientation; Judgment and Decision Making; Monitoring; Active Listening.

Education/Training Programs: Human Resources Management/Personnel Administration, General; Labor and Industrial Relations. **Related Knowledge/ Courses:** Personnel and Human Resources; Communications and Media; Sales and Marketing; Clerical; Law and Government; English Language.

Physical Therapist Aides

- Education/Training Required: Short-term on-the-job training
- Annual Earnings: $23,890
- Earnings Growth Potential: Low
- Growth: 36.3%
- Annual Job Openings: 2,340
- Self-Employed: 1.3%

Hottest Fields (with Growth): Social Assistance, Except Child Day Care (54.5%); Health Care (43.7%); Employment Services (20.0%).

Under close supervision of physical therapists or physical therapy assistants, perform delegated, selected, or routine tasks in specific situations. These duties include preparing patients and treatment areas. Clean and organize work areas and disinfect equipment after treatment. Administer active and passive manual therapeutic exercises, therapeutic massages, and heat, light, sound, water, or electrical modality treatments such as ultrasound. Instruct, motivate, safeguard, and assist patients practicing exercises and functional activities, under direction of medical staff. Record treatment given and equipment used. Confer with physical therapy staff or others to discuss and evaluate patient information for planning, modifying, and coordinating treatment. Observe patients during treatment to compile and evaluate data on patients' responses and progress, and report to physical therapists. Secure patients into or onto therapy equipment. Change linens such as bed sheets and pillow cases. Transport patients to and from treatment areas, using wheelchairs or providing standing support. Arrange treatment supplies to keep them in order. Maintain equipment and furniture to keep it in good working condition, including performing the assembly and disassembly of equipment and accessories. Assist patients to dress, undress, and put on and remove supportive devices such as braces, splints, and slings. Perform clerical duties such as taking inventory, ordering supplies, answering telephones, taking messages, and filling out forms. Administer traction to relieve neck and back pain, using intermittent and static traction equipment. Train patients to use orthopedic braces, prostheses, or supportive devices. Measure patient's range-of-joint motion, body parts, and vital signs to determine effects of treatments or for patient evaluations. Participate in patient care tasks such as assisting with passing food trays, feeding residents, or bathing residents on bed rest. Fit patients for orthopedic braces, prostheses, or supportive devices, adjusting fit as needed.

Career Cluster: 08 Health Science. **Pathway:** 08.1 Therapeutic Services.

Personality Type: Social-Realistic. **Skills:** None met the criteria.

Education/Training Program: Physical Therapy Technician/Assistant Training. **Related Knowledge/Courses:** Medicine and Dentistry; Therapy and Counseling; Customer and Personal Service; Psychology; Public Safety and Security.

Physical Therapist Assistants

- Education/Training Required: Associate degree
- Annual Earnings: $48,290
- Earnings Growth Potential: Medium
- Growth: 33.3%
- Annual Job Openings: 3,050
- Self-Employed: 1.3%

Hottest Fields (with Growth): Social Assistance, Except Child Day Care (49.3%); Health Care (41.1%); Employment Services (20.8%); Arts, Entertainment, and Recreation (20.0%); Educational Services (9.5%).

Assist physical therapists in providing physical therapy treatments and procedures. May, in accordance with state laws, assist in the development of treatment plans, carry out routine functions, document the progress of treatment, and modify specific treatments in accordance with patient status and within the scope of treatment plans established by physical therapists. Generally requires formal training. Instruct, motivate, safeguard, and assist patients as they practice exercises and functional activities. Observe patients during treatments to compile and evaluate data on their responses and progress; provide results to physical therapists in person or through progress notes. Confer with physical therapy staffs or others to discuss and evaluate patient information for planning, modifying, and coordinating treatment. Transport patients to and from treatment areas, lifting and transferring them according to positioning requirements. Secure patients into or onto therapy equipment. Administer active and passive manual therapeutic exercises; therapeutic massages; aquatic physical therapy; and heat, light, sound, and electrical modality treatments such as ultrasound. Communicate with or instruct caregivers and family members on patient therapeutic activities and treatment plans. Measure patients' ranges-of-joint motion, body parts, and vital signs to determine effects of treatments or for patient evaluations. Monitor operation of equipment and record use of equipment and administration of treatment. Fit patients for orthopedic braces, prostheses, and supportive devices such as crutches. Train patients in the use of orthopedic braces, prostheses, or supportive devices. Clean work areas and check and store equipment after treatments. Assist patients to dress; undress; or put on and remove supportive devices such as braces, splints, and slings. Attend or conduct continuing education courses, seminars, or in-service activities. Perform clerical duties such as taking inventory, ordering supplies, answering telephones, taking messages, and filling out forms.

Career Cluster: 08 Health Science. **Pathway:** 08.1 Therapeutic Services.

Personality Type: Social-Realistic-Investigative. **Skills:** Service Orientation; Systems Analysis; Quality Control Analysis; Systems Evaluation.

Education/Training Program: Physical Therapy Technician/Assistant Training.

Related Knowledge/Courses: Therapy and Counseling; Medicine and Dentistry; Psychology; Biology; Customer and Personal Service; Education and Training.

Physical Therapists

- Education/Training Required: Master's degree
- Annual Earnings: $74,480
- Earnings Growth Potential: Low
- Growth: 30.3%
- Annual Job Openings: 7,860
- Self-Employed: 8.0%

Hottest Fields (with Growth): Social Assistance, Except Child Day Care (47.6%); Health Care (40.6%); Arts, Entertainment, and Recreation (27.1%); Wholesale Trade (23.1%); Employment Services (20.8%).

Assess, plan, organize, and participate in rehabilitative programs that improve mobility, relieve pain, increase strength, and decrease or prevent deformity of patients suffering from disease or injury. Perform and document initial exams, evaluating data to identify problems and determine diagnoses prior to interventions. Plan, prepare, and carry out individually designed programs of physical treatment to maintain, improve, or restore physical functioning; alleviate pain; and prevent physical dysfunction in patients. Record prognoses, treatments, responses, and progresses in patients' charts or enter information into computers. Identify and document goals, anticipated progresses, and plans for reevaluation. Evaluate effects of treatments at various stages and adjust treatments to achieve maximum benefits. Administer manual exercises, massages, or traction to help relieve pain, increase patient strength, or decrease or prevent deformity or crippling. Test and measure patients' strength, motor development and function, sensory perception, functional capacity, and respiratory and circulatory efficiency and record data. Instruct patients and families in treatment procedures to be continued at home. Confer with patients, medical practitioners, and appropriate others to plan, implement, and assess intervention programs. Review physicians' referrals and patients' medical records to help determine diagnoses and physical therapy treatments required. Discharge patients from physical therapy when goals or projected outcomes have been attained and provide for appropriate follow-up care or referrals. Provide information to patients about proposed interventions, material risks, and expected benefits and any reasonable alternatives. Inform patients when diagnoses reveal findings outside the scope of physical therapy to treat and refer to appropriate practitioners. Provide educational information about physical therapy and physical therapists, injury prevention, ergonomics, and ways to promote health.

Career Cluster: 08 Health Science. **Pathway:** 08.3 Health Informatics.

Personality Type: Social-Investigative-Realistic. **Skills:** Systems Evaluation; Systems Analysis; Management of Personnel Resources; Service Orientation; Persuasion.

Education/Training Programs: Kinesiotherapy/Kinesiotherapist; Physical Therapy/Therapist. **Related Knowledge/Courses:** Therapy and Counseling; Medicine and Dentistry; Psychology; Education and Training; Biology; Customer and Personal Service.

Physician Assistants

- Education/Training Required: Master's degree
- Annual Earnings: $84,420
- Earnings Growth Potential: Low
- Growth: 39.0%
- Annual Job Openings: 4,280
- Self-Employed: 1.4%

Our sources did not provide separate job openings data for this occupation. The job openings listed here are shared with Anesthesiologist Assistants.

Hottest Fields (with Growth): Health Care (44.8%); Social Assistance, Except Child Day Care (40.0%); Scientific Research and Development Services (37.5%); Employment Services (36.7%); Educational Services (23.1%).

Under the supervision of physicians, provide health-care services typically performed by a physician. Conduct complete physicals, provide treatment, and counsel patients. May, in some cases, prescribe medication. Must graduate from an accredited educational program for physician assistants. Examine patients to obtain information about their physical conditions. Obtain, compile, and record patient medical data, including health history, progress notes, and results of physical examinations. Interpret diagnostic test results for deviations from normal. Make tentative diagnoses and decisions about management and treatment of patients. Prescribe therapy or medication with physician approval. Administer or order diagnostic tests, such as X-ray, electrocardiogram, and laboratory tests. Instruct and counsel patients about prescribed therapeutic regimens, normal growth and development, family planning, emotional problems of daily living, and health maintenance. Perform therapeutic procedures such as injections, immunizations, suturing and wound care, and infection management. Provide physicians with assistance during surgery or complicated medical procedures. Visit and observe patients on hospital rounds or house calls, updating charts, ordering therapy, and reporting back to physicians.

Career Cluster: 08 Health Science. **Pathway:** 08.2 Diagnostics Services.

Personality Type: Social-Investigative-Realistic. **Skills:** Systems Evaluation; Judgment and Decision Making; Service Orientation; Systems Analysis; Social Perceptiveness; Reading Comprehension; Persuasion; Negotiation; Instructing.

Education/Training Program: Physician Assistant Training. **Related Knowledge/ Courses:** Medicine and Dentistry; Biology; Therapy and Counseling; Psychology; Chemistry; Sociology and Anthropology.

Police and Sheriff's Patrol Officers

See Police Patrol Officers and Sheriffs and Deputy Sheriffs, described separately.

Police Patrol Officers

- Education/Training Required: Long-term on-the-job training
- Annual Earnings: $53,210
- Earnings Growth Potential: High
- Growth: 8.7%
- Annual Job Openings: 22,790
- Self-Employed: 0.0%

Our sources did not provide separate job openings data for this occupation. The job openings listed here are shared with Sheriffs and Deputy Sheriffs.

Hottest Fields (with Growth): Educational Services (30.3%); Health Care (12.4%).

Patrol assigned areas to enforce laws and ordinances, regulate traffic, control crowds, prevent crime, and arrest violators. Provide for public safety by maintaining order, responding to emergencies, protecting people and property, enforcing motor vehicle and criminal laws, and promoting good community relations. Monitor, note, report, and investigate suspicious persons and situations, safety hazards, and unusual or illegal activity in patrol area. Record facts to prepare reports that document incidents and activities. Identify, pursue, and arrest suspects and perpetrators of criminal acts. Patrol specific areas on foot, horseback, or motorized conveyance, responding promptly to calls for assistance. Review facts of incidents to determine whether criminal acts or statute violations were involved. Investigate traffic accidents and other accidents to determine causes and to determine whether crimes have been committed. Render aid to accident victims and other persons requiring first aid for physical injuries. Testify in court to present evidence or act as witness in traffic and criminal cases. Photograph or draw diagrams of crime or accident scenes and interview principals and eyewitnesses. Relay complaint and emergency-request information to appropriate agency dispatchers. Evaluate complaint and emergency-request information to determine response requirements. Process prisoners and prepare and maintain records of prisoner bookings and prisoner statuses during booking and pre-trial processes. Monitor traffic to ensure motorists observe traffic regulations and exhibit safe driving procedures. Issue citations or warnings to violators of motor vehicle ordinances. Direct traffic flow and reroute traffic during emergencies. Inform citizens of community services

© JIST Works

and recommend options to facilitate longer-term problem resolution. Provide road information to assist motorists. Act as official escorts at times, such as when leading funeral processions or firefighters.

Career Cluster: 12 Law, Public Safety, Corrections, and Security. **Pathway:** 12.4 Law Enforcement Services.

Personality Type: Realistic-Enterprising-Conventional. **Skills:** Negotiation; Persuasion; Service Orientation.

Education/Training Programs: Criminal Justice/Police Science; Criminalistics and Criminal Science. **Related Knowledge/Courses:** Psychology; Public Safety and Security; Law and Government; Customer and Personal Service; Therapy and Counseling; Sociology and Anthropology.

Preschool Teachers, Except Special Education

- Education/Training Required: Postsecondary vocational training
- Annual Earnings: $24,540
- Earnings Growth Potential: Low
- Growth: 19.0%
- Annual Job Openings: 17,830
- Self-Employed: 1.4%

Hottest Fields (with Growth): Computer Systems Design and Related Services (37.5%); Employment Services (24.3%); Child Day Care Services (22.8%); Health Care (21.0%); Social Assistance, Except Child Day Care (20.0%).

Instruct children (normally up to 5 years of age) in activities designed to promote social, physical, and intellectual growth needed for primary school in preschool, day care center, or other child development facility. May be required to hold state certification. Provide a variety of materials and resources for children to explore, manipulate, and use, both in learning activities and in imaginative play. Attend to children's basic needs by feeding them, dressing them, and changing their diapers. Establish and enforce rules for behavior and procedures for maintaining order. Read books to entire classes or to small groups. Teach basic skills such as color, shape, number, and letter recognition; personal hygiene; and social skills. Organize and lead activities designed to promote physical, mental, and social development, such as games, arts and crafts, music, storytelling, and field trips. Observe and evaluate children's performance, behavior, social development, and physical health. Meet with parents and guardians to discuss their children's progress and needs, determine their priorities for their children, and suggest ways that they can promote learning and development. Identify children showing signs of emotional, developmental, or health-related problems and discuss them with supervisors, parents or guardians, and child development specialists. Enforce all administration policies and rules governing students. Prepare materials and classrooms for class activities. Teach proper eating habits and personal hygiene.

Assimilate arriving children to the school environment by greeting them, helping them remove outerwear, and selecting activities of interest to them. Adapt teaching methods and instructional materials to meet students' varying needs and interests. Establish clear objectives for all lessons, units, and projects and communicate those objectives to children. Demonstrate activities to children. Arrange indoor and outdoor space to facilitate creative play, motor-skill activities, and safety.

Career Clusters: 05 Education and Training; 10 Human Services. **Pathways:** 05.3 Teaching/Training; 10.1 Early Childhood Development and Services.

Personality Type: Social-Artistic. **Skills:** Learning Strategies; Social Perceptiveness; Writing.

Education/Training Programs: Child Care and Support Services Management; Early Childhood Education and Teaching. **Related Knowledge/Courses:** Philosophy and Theology; Sociology and Anthropology; Psychology; Customer and Personal Service; Education and Training.

Production, Planning, and Expediting Clerks

- Education/Training Required: Moderate-term on-the-job training
- Annual Earnings: $41,560
- Earnings Growth Potential: Medium
- Growth: 1.5%
- Annual Job Openings: 7,410
- Self-Employed: 0.5%

Hottest Fields (with Growth): Management, Scientific, and Technical Consulting Services (85.3%); Computer Systems Design and Related Services (39.2%); Software Publishers (26.6%); Scientific Research and Development Services (24.0%); Employment Services (23.6%).

Coordinate and expedite the flow of work and materials within or between departments of an establishment according to production schedules.inventory levels, costs, and production problems. Examine documents, materials, and products, and monitor work processes to assess completeness, accuracy, and conformance to standards and specifications. Review documents such as production schedules, work orders, and staffing tables to determine personnel and materials requirements, and material priorities. Revise production schedules when required due to design changes, labor or material shortages, backlogs, or other interruptions, collaborating with management, marketing, sales, production, and engineering. Confer with department supervisors and other personnel to assess progress and discuss needed changes. Confer with establishment personnel, vendors, and customers to coordinate production and shipping activities, and to resolve complaints or eliminate delays. Record production data, including volume produced, consumption of raw materials, and quality control measures. Requisition and maintain inventories of materials and supplies necessary to meet production demands.

Calculate figures such as required amounts of labor and materials, manufacturing costs, and wages, using pricing schedules, adding machines, calculators, or computers. Distribute production schedules and work orders to departments. Compile information such as production rates and progress, materials inventories, materials used, and customer information, so that status reports can be completed. Arrange for delivery, assembly, and distribution of supplies and parts to expedite flow of materials and meet production schedules. Contact suppliers to verify shipment details. Maintain files such as maintenance records, bills of lading, and cost reports. Plan production commitments and timetables for business units, specific programs, and/or jobs, using sales forecasts.

Career Cluster: 16 Transportation, Distribution, and Logistics. **Pathway:** 16.3 Warehousing and Distribution Center Operations.

Personality Type: Conventional-Enterprising. **Skills:** Management of Material Resources; Operations Analysis; Management of Financial Resources; Systems Evaluation; Negotiation; Mathematics; Coordination; Persuasion; Active Learning.

Education/Training Program: Parts, Warehousing, and Inventory Management Operations. **Related Knowledge/Courses:** Production and Processing; Clerical; Computers and Electronics; Administration and Management; Mathematics; Customer and Personal Service.

Public Relations Specialists

- Education/Training Required: Bachelor's degree
- Annual Earnings: $51,960
- Earnings Growth Potential: High
- Growth: 24.0%
- Annual Job Openings: 13,130
- Self-Employed: 4.5%

Hottest Fields (with Growth): Management, Scientific, and Technical Consulting Services (104.0%); Computer Systems Design and Related Services (54.0%); Software Publishers (41.1%); Employment Services (36.0%); Social Assistance, Except Child Day Care (34.3%).

Engage in promoting or creating goodwill for individuals, groups, or organizations by writing or selecting favorable publicity material and releasing it through various communications media. May prepare and arrange displays and make speeches. Prepare or edit organizational publications for internal and external audiences, including employee newsletters and stockholders' reports. Respond to requests for information from the media or designate another appropriate spokesperson or information source. Establish and maintain cooperative relationships with representatives of community, consumer, employee, and public interest groups. Plan and direct development and communication of informational programs to maintain favorable public and stockholder perceptions of an organization's accomplishments and agenda. Confer with production and support personnel to produce or coordinate production of advertisements and promotions. Arrange public appearances, lectures, contests, or exhibits for clients to increase product and service awareness and to promote goodwill. Study the objectives, promotional policies, and needs of organizations to develop public relations strategies that will influence public opinion or promote ideas, products, and services. Consult with advertising agencies or staff to arrange promotional campaigns in all types of media for products, organizations, or individuals. Confer with other managers to identify trends and key group interests and concerns or to provide advice on business decisions. Coach client representatives in effective communication with the public and with employees.

Career Clusters: 03 Arts, Audio/Video Technology, and Communications; 04 Business, Management, and Administration. **Pathways:** 03.5 Journalism and Broadcasting; 04.1 Management.

Personality Type: Enterprising-Artistic-Social. **Skills:** Service Orientation; Management of Financial Resources; Persuasion; Writing; Negotiation; Social Perceptiveness; Judgment and Decision Making; Monitoring; Coordination.

Education/Training Programs: Family and Consumer Sciences/Human Sciences Communication; Health Communication; Political Communication; Public Relations/Image Management; Speech Communication and Rhetoric. **Related Knowledge/Courses:** Communications and Media; Sales and Marketing; English Language; Geography; Computers and Electronics; Customer and Personal Service.

Purchasing Agents, Except Wholesale, Retail, and Farm Products

- Education/Training Required: Long-term on-the-job training
- Annual Earnings: $54,810
- Earnings Growth Potential: Medium
- Growth: 13.9%
- Annual Job Openings: 11,860
- Self-Employed: 1.4%

Hottest Fields (with Growth): Management, Scientific, and Technical Consulting Services (104.0%); Computer Systems Design and Related Services (54.3%); Software Publishers (40.3%); Agriculture, Forestry, and Fishing (37.5%); Scientific Research and Development Services (37.2%).

Purchase machinery, equipment, tools, parts, supplies, or services necessary for the operation of an establishment. Purchase raw or semi-finished materials for manufacturing. Purchase the highest-quality merchandise at the lowest possible price and in correct amounts. Prepare purchase orders, solicit bid proposals, and review requisitions for goods and services. Research and evaluate suppliers based on price, quality, selection, service, support, availability, reliability, production and distribution capabilities, and the supplier's reputation and history. Analyze price proposals, financial reports, and other data and information to determine reasonable prices. Monitor and follow applicable laws and regulations. Negotiate, or renegotiate, and administer contracts with suppliers, vendors, and other representatives. Monitor shipments to ensure that goods come in on time and trace shipments and follow up on undelivered goods in the event of problems. Confer with staff, users, and vendors to discuss defective or unacceptable goods or services and determine corrective action. Evaluate and monitor contract performance to ensure compliance with contractual obligations and to determine need for changes. Maintain and review computerized or manual records of items purchased, costs, delivery, product performance, and inventories. Review catalogs, industry periodicals, directories, trade journals, and Internet sites and consult with other department personnel to locate necessary goods and services. Study sales records and inventory levels of current stock to develop strategic purchasing programs that facilitate employee access to supplies. Interview vendors and visit suppliers' plants and distribution centers to examine and learn about products, services, and prices. Arrange the payment of duty and freight charges. Hire, train, and/or supervise purchasing clerks, buyers, and expediters.

Career Cluster: 14 Marketing, Sales, and Service. **Pathway:** 14.3 Buying and Merchandising.

Personality Type: Conventional-Enterprising. **Skills:** Operations Analysis; Management of Material Resources; Management of Financial Resources; Writing; Mathematics; Speaking; Management of Personnel Resources; Judgment and Decision Making.

Education/Training Programs: Insurance; Merchandising and Buying Operations; Sales, Distribution, and Marketing Operations, General. **Related Knowledge/Courses:** Clerical; Economics and Accounting; Production and Processing; Administration and Management; Computers and Electronics; Communications and Media.

Refrigeration Mechanics and Installers

- Education/Training Required: Long-term on-the-job training
- Annual Earnings: $41,100
- Earnings Growth Potential: Medium
- Growth: 28.1%
- Annual Job Openings: 13,620
- Self-Employed: 15.5%

Our sources did not provide separate job openings data for this occupation. The job openings listed here are shared with Heating and Air Conditioning Mechanics and Installers.

Hottest Fields (with Growth): Construction (43.0%); Computer Systems Design and Related Services (40.0%); Scientific Research and Development Services (19.2%); Employment Services (16.7%); Social Assistance, Except Child Day Care (13.3%).

Install and repair industrial and commercial refrigerating systems. Braze or solder parts to repair defective joints and leaks. Observe and test system operation, using gauges and instruments. Test lines, components, and connections for leaks. Dismantle malfunctioning systems and test components, using electrical, mechanical, and pneumatic testing equipment. Adjust or replace worn or defective mechanisms and parts and reassemble repaired systems. Read blueprints to determine location, size, capacity, and type of components needed to build refrigeration system. Supervise and instruct assistants. Perform mechanical overhauls and refrigerant reclaiming. Install wiring to connect components to an electric power source. Cut, bend, thread, and connect pipe to functional components and water, power, or refrigeration system. Adjust valves according to specifications and charge system with proper type of refrigerant by pumping the specified gas or fluid into the system. Estimate, order, pick up, deliver, and install materials and supplies needed to maintain equipment in good working condition. Install expansion and control valves, using acetylene torches and wrenches. Mount compressor, condenser, and other components in specified locations on frames, using hand tools and acetylene welding equipment. Keep records of repairs and replacements made and causes of malfunctions. Schedule work with customers and initiate work orders, house requisitions, and orders from stock. Lay out reference points for installation of structural and functional components, using measuring instruments. Fabricate and assemble structural and functional components of refrigeration system, using hand tools, power tools, and welding equipment. Lift and align components into position, using hoist or block and tackle.

Career Cluster: 02 Architecture and Construction. **Pathways:** 02.2 Construction; 02.3 Maintenance/Operations.

Personality Type: Realistic-Conventional-Enterprising. **Skills:** Installation; Repairing; Equipment Maintenance; Operation Monitoring; Science; Systems Evaluation; Systems Analysis; Troubleshooting; Operation and Control.

Education/Training Programs: Heating, Air Conditioning, Ventilation and Refrigeration Maintenance Technology/Technician (HAC, HACR, HVAC, HVACR); Heating, Ventilation, Air Conditioning and Refrigeration Engineering Technology/Technician; Solar Energy Technology/Technician. **Related Knowledge/Courses:** Building and Construction; Mechanical; Engineering and Technology; Physics; Chemistry; Design.

Rehabilitation Counselors

- Education/Training Required: Master's degree
- Annual Earnings: $31,210

- Earnings Growth Potential: Low
- Growth: 18.9%
- Annual Job Openings: 5,070
- Self-Employed: 5.7%

Hottest Fields (with Growth): Social Assistance, Except Child Day Care (31.7%); Educational Services (20.4%); Child Day Care Services (14.3%); Advocacy, Grantmaking, and Civic Organizations (12.4%); Health Care (11.5%).

Counsel individuals to maximize the independence and employability of persons coping with personal, social, and vocational difficulties that result from birth defects, illness, disease, accidents, or the stress of daily life. Coordinate activities for residents of care and treatment facilities. Assess client needs and design and implement rehabilitation programs that may include personal and vocational counseling, training, and job placement. Monitor and record clients' progress in order to ensure that goals and objectives are met. Confer with clients to discuss their options and goals so that rehabilitation programs and plans for accessing needed services can be developed. Prepare and maintain records and case files, including documentation such as clients' personal and eligibility information, services provided, narratives of client contacts, and relevant correspondence. Arrange for physical, mental, academic, vocational, and other evaluations to obtain information for assessing clients' needs and developing rehabilitation plans. Analyze information from interviews, educational and medical records, consultation with other professionals, and diagnostic evaluations to assess clients' abilities, needs, and eligibility for services. Develop rehabilitation plans that fit clients' aptitudes, education levels, physical abilities, and career goals. Maintain close contact with clients during job training and placements to resolve problems and evaluate placement adequacy. Locate barriers to client employment, such as inaccessible work sites, inflexible schedules, and transportation problems, and work with clients to develop strategies for overcoming these barriers. Develop and maintain relationships with community referral sources such as schools and community groups. Arrange for on-site job coaching or assistive devices such as specially equipped wheelchairs in order to help clients adapt to work or school environments. Confer with physicians, psychologists, occupational therapists, and other professionals to develop and implement client rehabilitation programs. Develop diagnostic procedures for determining clients' needs. Participate in job development and placement programs, contacting prospective employers, placing clients in jobs, and evaluating the success of placements.

Career Cluster: 08 Health Science. **Pathway:** 08.3 Health Informatics.

Personality Type: Social-Investigative. **Skills:** Management of Financial Resources; Social Perceptiveness; Writing; Service Orientation; Monitoring; Coordination; Speaking; Judgment and Decision Making.

Education/Training Programs: Assistive/Augmentative Technology and Rehabilitation Engineering; Vocational Rehabilitation Counseling/Counselor. **Related Knowledge/Courses:** No data available.

Retail Salespersons

- Education/Training Required: Short-term on-the-job training
- Annual Earnings: $20,260
- Earnings Growth Potential: Very low
- Growth: 8.3%
- Annual Job Openings: 162,690
- Self-Employed: 3.4%

Hottest Fields (with Growth): Management, Scientific, and Technical Consulting Services (93.3%); Computer Systems Design and Related Services (51.9%); Social Assistance, Except Child Day Care (34.8%); Broadcasting (30.8%); Educational Services (29.5%).

Sell merchandise, such as furniture, motor vehicles, appliances, or apparel, in a retail establishment. Greet customers and ascertain what each customer wants or needs. Open and close cash registers, performing tasks such as counting money; separating charge slips, coupons, and vouchers; balancing cash drawers; and making deposits. Maintain knowledge of current sales and promotions, policies regarding payment and exchanges, and security practices. Compute sales prices and total purchases and receive and process cash or credit payment. Watch for and recognize security risks and thefts and know how to prevent or handle these situations. Maintain records related to sales. Recommend, select, and help locate or obtain merchandise based on customer needs and desires. Answer questions regarding the store and its merchandise. Describe merchandise and explain use, operation, and care of merchandise to customers. Prepare sales slips or sales contracts. Ticket, arrange, and display merchandise to promote sales. Place special orders or call other stores to find desired items. Demonstrate use or operation of merchandise. Clean shelves, counters, and tables. Exchange merchandise for customers and accept returns. Bag or package purchases and wrap gifts. Help customers try on or fit merchandise. Inventory stock and requisition new stock. Prepare merchandise for purchase or rental. Sell or arrange for delivery, insurance, financing, or service contracts for merchandise. Estimate and quote trade-in allowances. Estimate cost of repair or alteration of merchandise. Estimate quantity and cost of merchandise required, such as paint or floor covering. Rent merchandise to customers.

Career Clusters: 01 Agriculture, Food, and Natural Resources; 14 Marketing, Sales, and Service. **Pathways:** 01.2 Plant Systems; 14.2 Professional Sales and Marketing; 14.3 Buying and Merchandising.

Personality Type: Enterprising-Conventional. **Skills:** None met the criteria.

Education/Training Programs: Floriculture/Floristry Operations and Management; Retailing and Retail Operations; Sales, Distribution, and Marketing Operations, General; Selling Skills and Sales Operations. **Related Knowledge/ Courses:** Sales and Marketing; Customer and Personal Service; Communications and Media; Psychology.

Sales Representatives, Wholesale and Manufacturing, Technical and Scientific Products

- Education/Training Required: Work experience in a related occupation
- Annual Earnings: $71,340
- Earnings Growth Potential: High
- Growth: 9.7%
- Annual Job Openings: 14,230
- Self-Employed: 3.6%

Our sources did not provide separate job openings data for this occupation. The job openings listed here are shared with Solar Sales Representatives and Assessors.

Hottest Fields (with Growth): Management, Scientific, and Technical Consulting Services (85.8%); Computer Systems Design and Related Services (40.3%); Software Publishers (28.3%); Construction (25.9%); Scientific Research and Development Services (25.4%).

Sell goods for wholesalers or manufacturers where technical or scientific knowledge is required in such areas as biology, engineering, chemistry, and electronics that is normally obtained from at least two years of postsecondary education. Contact new and existing customers to discuss their needs and to explain how these needs could be met by specific products and services. Answer customers' questions about products, prices, availability, product uses, and credit terms. Quote prices, credit terms, and other bid specifications. Emphasize product features based on analyses of customers' needs and on technical knowledge of product capabilities and limitations. Negotiate prices and terms of sales and service agreements. Maintain customer records, using automated systems. Identify prospective customers by using business directories, following leads from existing clients, participating in organizations and clubs, and attending trade shows and conferences. Prepare sales contracts for orders obtained and submit orders for processing. Select the correct products or assist customers in making product selections based on customers' needs, product specifications, and applicable regulations. Collaborate with colleagues to exchange information such as selling strategies and marketing information. Prepare sales presentations and proposals that explain product specifications and applications. Provide customers with ongoing technical support. Demonstrate and explain the operation and use of products. Inform customers of estimated delivery schedules, service contracts, warranties, or other information pertaining to purchased products. Attend sales and trade meetings and read related publications in order to obtain information about market conditions, business trends, and industry developments. Visit establishments to evaluate needs and to promote product or service sales. Complete expense reports, sales reports, and other paperwork.

Career Cluster: 14 Marketing, Sales, and Service. **Pathway:** 14.2 Professional Sales and Marketing.

Personality Type: Enterprising-Conventional. **Skills:** Persuasion; Negotiation; Science; Management of Financial Resources; Service Orientation; Coordination; Operations Analysis; Social Perceptiveness; Active Listening.

Education/Training Programs: Business, Management, Marketing, and Related Support Services, Other; Selling Skills and Sales Operations. **Related Knowledge/Courses:** Sales and Marketing; Customer and Personal Service; Production and Processing; Administration and Management; Computers and Electronics; Transportation.

Security and Fire Alarm Systems Installers

- Education/Training Required: Postsecondary vocational training
- Annual Earnings: $37,710
- Earnings Growth Potential: Low
- Growth: 24.8%
- Annual Job Openings: 2,780
- Self-Employed: 6.3%

Hottest Fields (with Growth): Construction (33.0%); Employment Services (22.9%); Educational Services (12.1%); Wholesale Trade (4.0%).

Install, program, maintain, and repair security and fire alarm wiring and equipment. Ensure that work is in accordance with relevant codes. Examine systems to locate problems such as loose connections or broken insulation. Test backup batteries, keypad programming, sirens, and all security features in order to ensure proper functioning, and to diagnose malfunctions. Mount and fasten control panels, door and window contacts, sensors, and video cameras, and attach electrical and telephone wiring in order to connect components. Install, maintain, or repair security systems, alarm devices, and related equipment, following blueprints of electrical layouts and building plans. Inspect installation sites and study work orders, building plans, and installation manuals in order to determine materials requirements and installation procedures. Feed cables through access holes, roof spaces, and cavity walls to reach fixture outlets; then position and terminate cables, wires and strapping. Adjust sensitivity of units based on room structures and manufacturers' recommendations, using programming keypads. Test and repair circuits and sensors, following wiring and system specifications. Drill holes for wiring in wall studs, joists, ceilings, and floors. Demonstrate systems for customers and explain details such as the causes and consequences of false alarms. Consult with clients to assess risks and to determine security requirements. Keep informed of new products and developments. Mount raceways and conduits and fasten wires to wood framing, using staplers. Prepare documents such as invoices and warranties. Provide customers with cost estimates for equipment installation. Order replacement parts.

Career Cluster: 02 Architecture and Construction. **Pathways:** 02.2 Construction; 02.3 Maintenance/Operations.

Personality Type: Realistic-Conventional. **Skills:** Installation; Repairing; Troubleshooting; Equipment Maintenance; Systems Evaluation; Technology Design; Operations Analysis; Programming.

Education/Training Programs: Electrician; Security System Installation, Repair, and Inspection Technology/Technician. **Related Knowledge/Courses:** Telecommunications; Building and Construction; Mechanical; Computers and Electronics; Public Safety and Security; Design.

Self-Enrichment Education Teachers

- Education/Training Required: Work experience in a related occupation
- Annual Earnings: $36,440
- Earnings Growth Potential: High
- Growth: 32.0%
- Annual Job Openings: 12,030
- Self-Employed: 17.3%

Hottest Fields (with Growth): Management, Scientific, and Technical Consulting Services (84.2%); Educational Services (49.6%); Computer Systems Design and Related Services (41.7%); Air Transportation (30.0%); Employment Services (24.7%).

Teach or instruct courses other than those that normally lead to an occupational objective or degree. Courses may include self-improvement, nonvocational, and nonacademic subjects. Teaching may or may not take place in a traditional educational institution. Adapt teaching methods and instructional materials to meet students' varying needs and interests. Conduct classes, workshops, and demonstrations and provide individual instruction to teach topics and skills such as cooking, dancing, writing, physical fitness, photography, personal finance, and flying. Monitor students' performance to make suggestions for improvement and to ensure that they satisfy course standards, training requirements, and objectives. Observe students to determine qualifications, limitations, abilities, interests, and other individual characteristics. Instruct students individually and in groups, using various teaching methods such as lectures, discussions, and demonstrations. Establish clear objectives for all lessons, units, and projects and communicate those objectives to students. Instruct and monitor students in use and care of equipment and materials to prevent injury and damage. Prepare students for further development by encouraging them to explore learning opportunities and to persevere with challenging tasks. Prepare materials and classrooms for class activities. Enforce policies and rules governing students. Plan and conduct activities for a balanced program of instruction, demonstration, and work time that provides students with opportunities to observe, question, and investigate. Prepare instructional program objectives, outlines, and lesson plans. Maintain accurate and complete student records as required by administrative policy. Participate in publicity planning and student recruitment. Plan and supervise class projects, field trips, visits by guest speakers, contests, or other experiential activities and guide students in learning from those activities. Attend professional meetings, conferences, and workshops in order to maintain and improve professional competence. Meet with other instructors to discuss individual students and their progress.

Career Cluster: 05 Education and Training. **Pathway:** 05.3 Teaching/Training.

Personality Type: Social-Artistic-Enterprising. **Skills:** Instructing; Learning Strategies; Social Perceptiveness; Service Orientation; Monitoring; Speaking; Persuasion; Time Management.

Education/Training Program: Adult and Continuing Education and Teaching. **Related Knowledge/Courses:** Fine Arts; Education and Training; Psychology; Customer and Personal Service; Sales and Marketing; Administration and Management.

Septic Tank Servicers and Sewer Pipe Cleaners

- Education/Training Required: Moderate-term on-the-job training
- Annual Earnings: $33,350
- Earnings Growth Potential: Medium
- Growth: 23.8%
- Annual Job Openings: 1,320
- Self-Employed: 4.5%

Hottest Fields (with Growth): Construction (37.8%); Utilities (25.0%).

Clean and repair septic tanks, sewer lines, or drains. May patch walls and partitions of tank, replace damaged drain tile, or repair breaks in underground piping. Drive trucks to transport crews, materials, and equipment. Communicate with supervisors and other workers, using equipment such as wireless phones, pagers, or radio telephones. Prepare and keep records of actions taken, including maintenance and repair work. Operate sewer cleaning equipment, including power rodders, high velocity water jets, sewer flushers, bucket machines, wayne balls, and vac-alls. Ensure that repaired sewer line joints are tightly sealed before backfilling begins. Withdraw cables from pipes and examine them for evidence of mud, roots, grease, and other deposits indicating broken or clogged sewer lines. Install rotary knives on flexible cables mounted on machine reels according to the diameters of pipes to be cleaned. Measure excavation sites, using plumbers' snakes, tapelines, or lengths of cutting heads within sewers, and mark areas for digging. Locate problems, using specially designed equipment, and mark where digging must occur to reach damaged tanks or pipes. Start machines to feed revolving cables or rods into openings, stopping machines and changing knives to conform to pipe sizes. Clean and repair septic tanks; sewer lines; or related structures such as manholes, culverts, and catch basins. Service, adjust, and make minor repairs to equipment, machines, and attachments. Inspect manholes to locate sewer line stoppages. Cut damaged sections of pipe with cutters; remove broken sections from ditches; and replace pipe sections, using pipe sleeves. Dig out sewer lines manually, using shovels. Break asphalt and other pavement so that pipes can be accessed, using airhammers, picks, and shovels. Cover repaired pipes with dirt and pack backfilled excavations, using air and gasoline tampers. Requisition or order tools and equipment. Rotate cleaning rods manually, using turning pins. Clean and disinfect domestic basements and other areas flooded by sewer stoppages.

Career Cluster: 02 Architecture and Construction. **Pathway:** 02.2 Construction.

Personality Type: Realistic. **Skills:** Equipment Maintenance; Repairing; Installation; Operation Monitoring; Operation and Control; Troubleshooting; Systems Analysis; Management of Material Resources.

Education/Training Program: Plumbing Technology/Plumber. **Related Knowledge/Courses:** Building and Construction; Mechanical; Sales and Marketing; Transportation; Production and Processing; Customer and Personal Service.

Sheriffs and Deputy Sheriffs

- Education/Training Required: Long-term on-the-job training
- Annual Earnings: $53,210
- Earnings Growth Potential: High
- Growth: 8.7%
- Annual Job Openings: 22,790
- Self-Employed: 0.0%

Our sources did not provide separate job openings data for this occupation. The job openings listed here are shared with Police Patrol Officers.

Hottest Fields (with Growth): Educational Services (30.3%); Health Care (12.4%).

Enforce law and order in rural or unincorporated districts or serve legal processes of courts. May patrol courthouse, guard court or grand jury, or escort defendants. Drive vehicles or patrol specific areas to detect law violators, issue citations, and make arrests. Investigate illegal or suspicious activities. Verify that the proper legal charges have been made against law offenders. Execute arrest warrants, locating and taking persons into custody. Record daily activities and submit logs and other related reports and paperwork to appropriate authorities. Patrol and guard courthouses, grand jury rooms, or assigned areas to provide security, enforce laws, maintain order, and arrest violators. Notify patrol units to take violators into custody or to provide needed assistance or medical aid. Place people in protective custody. Serve statements of claims, subpoenas, summonses, jury summonses, orders to pay alimony, and other court orders. Take control of accident scenes to maintain traffic flow, to assist accident victims, and to investigate causes. Question individuals entering secured areas to determine their business, directing and rerouting individuals as necessary. Transport or escort prisoners and defendants en route to courtrooms, prisons or jails, attorneys' offices, or medical facilities. Locate and confiscate real or personal property, as directed by court order. Manage jail operations and tend to jail inmates.

Career Cluster: 12 Law, Public Safety, Corrections, and Security. **Pathways:** 12.3 Security and Protective Services; 12.4 Law Enforcement Services.

Personality Type: Enterprising-Realistic-Social. **Skills:** Negotiation; Persuasion; Social Perceptiveness; Service Orientation; Equipment Selection; Complex Problem Solving; Judgment and Decision Making; Coordination; Writing; Equipment Maintenance.

Education/Training Programs: Criminal Justice/Police Science; Criminalistics and Criminal Science. **Related Knowledge/Courses:** Public Safety and Security; Law and Government; Telecommunications; Psychology; Therapy and Counseling; Philosophy and Theology.

Social and Human Service Assistants

- Education/Training Required: Moderate-term on-the-job training
- Annual Earnings: $27,940
- Earnings Growth Potential: Low
- Growth: 22.6%
- Annual Job Openings: 15,390
- Self-Employed: 0.3%

Hottest Fields (with Growth): Management, Scientific, and Technical Consulting Services (100.0%); Social Assistance, Except Child Day Care (44.8%); Employment Services (27.7%); Scientific Research and Development Services (19.4%); Educational Services (17.9%).

Assist professionals from a wide variety of fields such as psychology, rehabilitation, or social work to provide client services, as well as support for families. May assist clients in identifying available benefits and social and community services and help clients obtain them. May assist social workers with developing, organizing, and conducting programs to prevent and resolve

problems relevant to substance abuse, human relationships, rehabilitation, or adult daycare. Keep records and prepare reports for owner or management concerning visits with clients. Submit reports and review reports or problems with superior. Interview individuals and family members to compile information on social, educational, criminal, institutional, or drug histories. Provide information and refer individuals to public or private agencies or community services for assistance. Consult with supervisors concerning programs for individual families. Advise clients regarding food stamps, child care, food, money management, sanitation, or housekeeping. Oversee day-to-day group activities of residents in institution. Visit individuals in homes or attend group meetings to provide information on agency services, requirements, and procedures. Monitor free, supplementary meal program to ensure cleanliness of facility and that eligibility guidelines are met for persons receiving meals. Meet with youth groups to acquaint them with consequences of delinquent acts. Assist in planning of food budgets, using charts and sample budgets. Transport and accompany clients to shopping areas or to appointments, using automobiles. Assist in locating housing for displaced individuals. Observe and discuss meal preparation and suggest alternate methods of food preparation. Observe clients' food selections and recommend alternative economical and nutritional food choices. Explain rules established by owner or management, such as sanitation and maintenance requirements or parking regulations. Care for children in clients' homes during clients' appointments.

Career Cluster: 08 Health Science. **Pathway:** 08.1 Therapeutic Services.

Personality Type: Conventional-Social-Enterprising. **Skills:** Social Perceptiveness; Service Orientation; Systems Analysis; Systems Evaluation.

Education/Training Program: Mental and Social Health Services and Allied Professions, Other. **Related Knowledge/Courses:** No data available.

Special Education Teachers, Preschool, Kindergarten, and Elementary School

- Education/Training Required: Bachelor's degree
- Annual Earnings: $50,950
- Earnings Growth Potential: Low
- Growth: 19.6%
- Annual Job Openings: 10,290
- Self-Employed: 0.2%

Hottest Fields (with Growth): Social Assistance, Except Child Day Care (56.8%); Health Care (48.6%); Child Day Care Services (22.8%); Educational Services (18.5%).

Teach elementary and preschool school subjects to educationally and physically handicapped students. Includes teachers who specialize and work with

audibly and visually handicapped students and those who teach basic academic and life processes skills to the mentally impaired. Instruct students in academic subjects, using a variety of techniques such as phonetics, multisensory learning, and repetition to reinforce learning and to meet students' varying needs and interests. Employ special educational strategies and techniques during instruction to improve the development of sensory- and perceptual-motor skills, language, cognition, and memory. Teach socially acceptable behavior, employing techniques such as behavior modification and positive reinforcement. Modify the general education curriculum for special-needs students based upon a variety of instructional techniques and technologies. Meet with parents and guardians to discuss their children's progress and to determine their priorities for their children and their resource needs. Plan and conduct activities for a balanced program of instruction, demonstration, and work time that provides students with opportunities to observe, question, and investigate. Establish and enforce rules for behavior and policies and procedures to maintain order among the students for whom they are responsible. Confer with parents, administrators, testing specialists, social workers, and professionals to develop individual educational plans designed to promote students' educational, physical, and social development. Maintain accurate and complete student records and prepare reports on children and activities as required by laws, district policies, and administrative regulations. Establish clear objectives for all lessons, units, and projects and communicate those objectives to students. Develop and implement strategies to meet the needs of students with a variety of handicapping conditions. Prepare classrooms for class activities and provide a variety of materials and resources for children to explore, manipulate, and use, both in learning activities and imaginative play. Confer with parents or guardians, teachers, counselors, and administrators to resolve students' behavioral and academic problems.

Career Cluster: 05 Education and Training. **Pathway:** 05.3 Teaching/Training.

Personality Type: Social-Artistic. **Skills:** Learning Strategies; Instructing; Social Perceptiveness; Monitoring; Negotiation; Time Management; Coordination; Writing; Speaking.

Education/Training Programs: Education/Teaching of Individuals with Autism; Education/Teaching of Individuals with Emotional Disturbances; Education/Teaching of Individuals with Hearing Impairments Including Deafness; Education/Teaching of Individuals with Mental Retardation; Education/Teaching of Individuals with Multiple Disabilities; Education/Teaching of Individuals with Orthopedic and Other Physical Health Impairments; Education/Teaching of Individuals with Specific Learning Disabilities; others. **Related Knowledge/Courses:** Psychology; History and Archeology; Therapy and Counseling; Geography; Philosophy and Theology; Sociology and Anthropology.

Speech-Language Pathologists

- Education/Training Required: Master's degree
- Annual Earnings: $65,090
- Earnings Growth Potential: Low
- Growth: 18.5%
- Annual Job Openings: 4,380
- Self-Employed: 9.0%

Hottest Fields (with Growth): Social Assistance, Except Child Day Care (43.4%); Health Care (41.4%); Employment Services (26.1%); Child Day Care Services (14.3%); Advocacy, Grantmaking, and Civic Organizations (10.0%).

Assess and treat persons with speech, language, voice, and fluency disorders. May select alternative communication systems and teach their use. May perform research related to speech and language problems. Monitor patients' progress and adjust treatments accordingly. Evaluate hearing and speech/language test results and medical or background information to diagnose and plan treatment for speech, language, fluency, voice, and swallowing disorders. Administer hearing or speech and language evaluations, tests, or examinations to patients to collect information on type and degree of impairments, using written and oral tests and special instruments. Record information on the initial evaluation, treatment, progress, and discharge of clients. Develop and implement treatment plans for problems such as stuttering, delayed language, swallowing disorders, and inappropriate pitch or harsh voice problems based on own assessments and recommendations of physicians, psychologists, or social workers. Develop individual or group programs in schools to deal with speech or language problems. Instruct clients in techniques for more effective communication, including sign language, lip reading, and voice improvement. Teach clients to control or strengthen tongue, jaw, face muscles, and breathing mechanisms. Develop speech exercise programs to reduce disabilities. Consult with and advise educators or medical staff on speech or hearing topics, such as communication strategies or speech and language stimulation. Instruct patients and family members in strategies to cope with or avoid communication-related misunderstandings. Design, develop, and employ alternative diagnostic or communication devices and strategies. Conduct lessons and direct educational or therapeutic games to assist teachers dealing with speech problems. Refer clients to additional medical or educational services if needed.

Career Cluster: 08 Health Science. **Pathway:** 08.1 Therapeutic Services.

Personality Type: Social-Investigative-Artistic. **Skills:** Learning Strategies; Instructing; Social Perceptiveness; Speaking; Monitoring; Service Orientation; Reading Comprehension; Active Learning; Time Management; Writing.

Education/Training Programs: Audiology/Audiologist and Speech-Language Pathology/Pathologist; Communication Disorders Sciences and Services, Other;

Communication Disorders, General; Communication Sciences and Disorders, General; Speech-Language Pathology/Pathologist. **Related Knowledge/Courses:** Therapy and Counseling; English Language; Psychology; Sociology and Anthropology; Education and Training; Medicine and Dentistry.

Survey Researchers

- Education/Training Required: Bachelor's degree
- Annual Earnings: $35,380
- Earnings Growth Potential: High
- Growth: 30.3%
- Annual Job Openings: 1,340
- Self-Employed: 6.7%

Hottest Fields (with Growth): Management, Scientific, and Technical Consulting Services (94.7%); Employment Services (49.4%); Scientific Research and Development Services (43.1%); Advocacy, Grantmaking, and Civic Organizations (36.1%); Educational Services (28.1%).

Design or conduct surveys. May supervise interviewers who conduct the survey in person or over the telephone. May present survey results to client. Prepare and present summaries and analyses of survey data, including tables, graphs, and fact sheets that describe survey techniques and results. Consult with clients in order to identify survey needs and any specific requirements, such as special samples. Analyze data from surveys, old records, and/or case studies, using statistical software programs. Review, classify, and record survey data in preparation for computer analysis. Conduct research in order to gather information about survey topics. Conduct surveys and collect data, using methods such as interviews, questionnaires, focus groups, market analysis surveys, public opinion polls, literature reviews, and file reviews. Collaborate with other researchers in the planning, implementation, and evaluation of surveys. Direct and review the work of staff members, including survey support staff and interviewers who gather survey data. Monitor and evaluate survey progress and performance, using sample disposition reports and response rate calculations. Produce documentation of the questionnaire development process, data collection methods, sampling designs, and decisions related to sample statistical weighting. Determine and specify details of survey projects, including sources of information, procedures to be used, and the design of survey instruments and materials. Support, plan, and coordinate operations for single or multiple surveys. Direct updates and changes in survey implementation and methods. Hire and train recruiters and data collectors.

Career Clusters: 04 Business, Management, and Administration; 14 Marketing, Sales, and Service; 15 Science, Technology, Engineering, and Mathematics. **Pathways:** 04.1 Management; 14.5 Marketing Information Management and Research; 15.3 Science and Mathematics.

Personality Type: Investigative-Conventional-Enterprising. **Skills:** Management of Financial Resources; Management of Personnel Resources; Time Management; Writing; Persuasion; Complex Problem Solving; Mathematics; Active Learning; Operations Analysis; Judgment and Decision Making.

Education/Training Programs: Applied Economics; Business/Managerial Economics; Economics, General; Marketing Research. **Related Knowledge/ Courses:** No data available.

Telecommunications Equipment Installers and Repairers, Except Line Installers

- Education/Training Required: Postsecondary vocational training
- Annual Earnings: $55,560
- Earnings Growth Potential: High
- Growth: –0.2%
- Annual Job Openings: 3,560
- Self-Employed: 4.0%

Hottest Fields (with Growth): Management, Scientific, and Technical Consulting Services (84.7%); Computer Systems Design and Related Services (40.1%); Construction (35.3%); Software Publishers (28.6%); Scientific Research and Development Services (25.8%).

Set up, rearrange, or remove switching and dialing equipment used in central offices. Service or repair telephones and other communication equipment on customers' properties. May install equipment in new locations or install wiring and telephone jacks in buildings under construction. Note differences in wire and cable colors so that work can be performed correctly. Test circuits and components of malfunctioning telecommunications equipment to isolate sources of malfunctions, using test meters, circuit diagrams, polarity probes, and other hand tools. Test repaired, newly installed, or updated equipment to ensure that it functions properly and conforms to specifications, using test equipment and observation. Drive crew trucks to and from work areas. Inspect equipment on a regular basis to ensure proper functioning. Repair or replace faulty equipment such as defective and damaged telephones, wires, switching system components, and associated equipment. Remove and remake connections to change circuit layouts, following work orders or diagrams. Demonstrate equipment to customers, explain how it is to be used, and respond to any inquiries or complaints. Analyze test readings, computer printouts, and trouble reports to determine equipment repair needs and required repair methods. Adjust or modify equipment to enhance equipment performance or to respond to customer requests. Remove loose wires and other debris after work is completed. Request support from technical service centers when on-site procedures fail to solve installation or maintenance problems. Communicate with bases, using telephones or two-way radios, to receive instructions or technical advice or to report equipment status. Assemble and install communication equipment such as data and telephone communication lines, wiring, switching equipment, wiring frames, power apparatus, computer systems, and networks. Collaborate with other workers to locate and correct malfunctions.

Career Cluster: 03 Arts, Audio/Video Technology, and Communications. **Pathway:** 03.6 Telecommunications.

Personality Type: Realistic-Investigative-Conventional. **Skills:** Installation; Repairing; Troubleshooting; Technology Design; Equipment Selection; Systems Analysis; Quality Control Analysis; Equipment Maintenance; Operations Analysis.

Education/Training Program: Communications Systems Installation and Repair Technology. **Related Knowledge/Courses:** Telecommunications; Mechanical; Computers and Electronics; Engineering and Technology; Design; Public Safety and Security.

Training and Development Specialists

- Education/Training Required: Work experience plus degree
- Annual Earnings: $52,120
- Earnings Growth Potential: High
- Growth: 23.3%
- Annual Job Openings: 10,710
- Self-Employed: 1.6%

Hottest Fields (with Growth): Management, Scientific, and Technical Consulting Services (103.9%); Computer Systems Design and Related Services (54.3%); Software Publishers (41.3%); Social Assistance, Except Child Day Care (36.2%); Employment Services (35.9%).

Conduct training and development programs for employees. Monitor, evaluate, and record training activities and program effectiveness. Offer specific training programs to help workers maintain or improve job skills. Assess training needs through surveys; interviews with employees; focus groups; or consultation with managers, instructors, or customer representatives. Develop alternative training methods if expected improvements are not seen. Organize and develop, or obtain, training procedure manuals and guides and course materials such as handouts and visual materials. Present information, using a variety of instructional techniques and formats such as role playing, simulations, team exercises, group discussions, videos, and lectures. Evaluate training materials prepared by instructors, such as outlines, text, and handouts. Design, plan, organize, and direct orientation and training for employees or customers of industrial or commercial establishments. Monitor training costs to ensure budget is not exceeded and prepare budget reports to justify expenditures. Select and assign instructors to conduct training. Schedule classes based on availability of classrooms, equipment, and instructors. Keep up with developments in their individual areas of expertise by reading current journals, books, and magazine articles. Supervise instructors, evaluate instructor performances, and refer instructors to classes for skill development. Coordinate recruitment and placement of training program participants. Attend meetings and seminars to obtain information for use in training programs or to inform management of training program statuses. Negotiate contracts with clients, including desired training outcomes, fees, and expenses.

Career Cluster: 04 Business, Management, and Administration. **Pathway:** 04.3 Human Resources.

Personality Type: Social-Artistic-Conventional. **Skills:** Systems Evaluation; Systems Analysis; Learning Strategies; Management of Personnel Resources; Writing; Negotiation; Instructing.

Education/Training Programs: Human Resources Management/Personnel Administration, General; Organizational Behavior Studies. **Related Knowledge/ Courses:** Education and Training; Sociology and Anthropology; Sales and Marketing; Clerical; Personnel and Human Resources; Psychology.

Where the Information Comes From and What It Means

The information in this book came mostly from databases and publications created by the U.S. Department of Labor:

- The Bureau of Labor Statistics (BLS) provided growth-projection figures for industries and for the occupations within them. It also provided average earnings figures of occupations, both industry-wide and within specific industries. These figures are reported under a classifying system called Standard Occupational Classification (SOC), which organizes the U.S. workforce into approximately 800 job titles. Some other information reported under SOC titles included figures on the number of self-employed workers in each job and on the level of education required.

- Additional information was obtained from the O*NET (Occupational Information Network) database, which is now the primary source of detailed information on occupations. The Labor Department updates O*NET regularly, and we used the most recent version available: O*NET release 14. Data from O*NET indicated the personality types associated with jobs, as well as the major work tasks, important skills, and types of knowledge. O*NET uses a slightly different set of job titles than SOC, and the two do not always match precisely. In a few cases, data is not available about each of these topics for every occupation. Nevertheless, the information reported here is the most reliable data available.

- Information in chapter 3 about industry trends is derived from a Web-only publication of the Department of Labor, the *Career Guide to Industries.*

- The Office of Vocational and Adult Education (OVAE) in the U.S. Department of Education matched occupations to educational programs, career clusters, and pathways.

- The Classification of Instructional Programs, a system developed by the U.S. Department of Education, provided the titles of the education or training programs related to each job.

Understand the Limits of the Data in This Book

This book uses the most reliable and up-to-date information available on earnings, projected growth, number of openings, and other topics. The earnings data came from the

U.S. Department of Labor's Bureau of Labor Statistics. As you look at the figures, keep in mind that they are estimates. They give you a general idea about the number of workers employed, annual earnings, rate of job growth, and annual job openings.

Understand that a problem with such data is that it describes an average. For example, the yearly earnings information in this book is the average annual pay received as of May 2009 by people in various job titles (actually, it is the median annual pay, which means that half earned more and half less). This single figure does not indicate how much earnings may vary. For example, people who are new to the occupation or with only a few years of work experience often earn much less than the median amount. People who live in rural areas or who work for smaller employers typically earn less than those who do similar work in cities (where the cost of living is higher) or for bigger employers. People in certain areas of the country earn less than those in others.

Most of the information in this book, like the earnings figures, represents averages. Often you can find a niche job within an occupation that pays more, uses a different set of skills, has different work conditions, or differs in some other way from the average.

Earnings

The employment security agency of each state gathers information on earnings for various jobs and forwards it to the U.S. Bureau of Labor Statistics. BLS reports earnings that are straight-time gross pay exclusive of premium pay. More specifically, the earnings figures include the job's base rate; cost-of-living allowances; guaranteed pay; hazardous-duty pay; incentive pay, including commissions and production bonuses; on-call pay; and tips. They do not include back pay, jury duty pay, overtime pay, severance pay, shift differentials, nonproduction bonuses, or tuition reimbursements. Also, self-employed workers are not included in the estimates, and they can be a significant segment in certain occupations.

In addition to the earnings figures reported for each job in Part II, you'll find a statement of the job's Earnings Growth Potential. This statement represents the gap between the 10th percentile (the figure that exceeds the earnings of the lowest 10 percent of the workers) and the median. This information answers the question, "If I started at the wage level roughly expected for beginners and then got a raise that took me up to the median, how much of a pay boost (in percentage terms) would that be?" If this would be a big boost, the job has great potential for increasing your earnings as you gain experience and skills. If the boost would be small, you probably will need to move on to another occupation to improve your earnings substantially. Rather than use a percentage figure, which might be hard to hard to interpret, Part II uses a verbal tag to express the Earnings Growth Potential: "very low" when the percentage is less than 25%, "low" for 25%–35%, "medium" for 35%–40%, "high" for 40%–50%, and "very high" for any figure higher than 50%.

The BLS reports earnings using SOC titles, and sometimes more than one O*NET title links to a single SOC title. That's why, if you look at the earnings for Accountants and the earnings for Auditors, you'll find the same figure: $60,340. The BLS reports this figure for the occupation Accountants and Auditors. In reality, there probably is a difference in the earnings of these two kinds of financial professionals, but the single figure is the best information available.

Projected Growth and Number of Job Openings

This information comes from the Office of Occupational Statistics and Employment Projections, a program within the Bureau of Labor Statistics that develops information about projected trends in the nation's labor market for the next 10 years. The most recent projections available cover the years 2008 to 2018. The projections assume that there will be no major war, depression, or other economic upheaval. They do assume that recessions may occur, in keeping with the business cycles we have experienced for several decades, but because they cover 10 years, they are intended to provide an average of both the good times and the bad times.

Like the earnings figures, the figures on projected growth and job openings are reported according to the SOC classification, so again you will find that some of the SOC jobs listed in chapter 3 correspond to more than one O*NET job in Part II. In such cases, you'll find two or more Part II jobs with the same figure for projected growth and a footnote stating that these occupations *share* the number of openings listed.

While salary figures are fairly straightforward, you may not know what to make of job-growth figures. For example, is a projected growth of 15 percent good or bad? Keep in mind that the average (mean) growth projected for all occupations by the Bureau of Labor Statistics is 10.1 percent. One-quarter of the SOC occupations have a growth projection of 1.0 percent or lower. Growth of 9.7 percent is the median, meaning that half of the occupations have more, half less. Only one-quarter of the occupations have growth projected at more than 15.1 percent.

The 66 unique jobs in chapter 3 were chosen largely because they are expected to grow fast, and in fact they average 17.2 percent growth. (Within the fields covered in chapter 3, many of them are growing even faster.) One-quarter of these jobs have a growth projection of 15.0 percent or lower. Growth of 22.0 percent is the median, meaning that half of the occupations have more, half less. One-quarter of the occupations have growth projected at more than 30.3 percent.

The BLS projects an average of about 7,000 job openings per year for each of the 750 occupations that it studies, but for the 66 occupations included in chapter 3, the average is about 17,000 openings. The job ranked 16th for job openings has a figure of about 16,100 annual openings, the job ranked 33rd (the median) has about 9,800 openings projected, and the job ranked 50th has about 4,400 openings projected.

Perhaps you're wondering why we present figures on both job growth *and* number of openings. Aren't these two ways of saying the same thing? Actually, you need to know both. Consider the occupation Biomedical Engineers, which is projected to grow at the astonishing rate of 72.0 percent. There should be lots of opportunities in such a fast-growing job, right? Not exactly. This is a small occupation, with only about 16,050 people currently employed, so although it is growing rapidly, it will not create many new jobs (about 1,490 per year). Now consider General and Operations Managers. This occupation has a projected growth rate of –0.1 percent, which means it is expected to *shrink* slightly. Nevertheless, this is a huge occupation that employs 1.7 million workers, so although it is not growing, it is expected to take on more than 50,000 new workers each year as existing workers retire, die, or move on to other jobs. That's why you should pay attention to both of these economic indicators when you read the facts about jobs in this book.

Information Topics in Part II

Part II contains descriptions of 86 O*NET job titles related to the 65 SOC-taxonomy job titles listed in chapter 3. The job descriptions use a format that is informative yet compact and easy to read. They contain statistics such as earnings and projected percent of growth; lists such as major skills and work tasks; and key descriptors such as personality type and career cluster. Because the jobs in this section are arranged in alphabetical order, you can easily find a job that you've identified from chapter 3 and that you want to learn more about.

As discussed earlier in this appendix, we used the most current information from a variety of government sources to create the descriptions. Although we've tried to make the descriptions easy to understand, the list of elements within them and explanations of those elements may help you better understand and use the descriptions.

Here are some details on each of the major parts of the job descriptions you will find in Part II:

- **Job Title:** This is the job title for the job as defined by the U.S. Department of Labor and used in its O*NET database.

- **Data Elements:** The information comes from various U.S. Department of Labor and Department of Education databases, as explained elsewhere in this appendix. Note that the level of Education/Training Required is the *minimal* amount that is common. In occupations where use of technology is growing rapidly, such as nursing or electronics repair, this level may qualify you for only the lowest-level positions.

- **Hottest Fields:** As many as five fast-growing industries are listed here, with the percentage of growth projected for 2008–2018. To be included, the industry must be growing and have a workforce of more than 5,000 people in this occupation. Some industries not described in chapter 3 may be included.

- **Summary Description and Tasks:** The boldfaced sentence provides a summary description of the occupation. It is followed by a listing of tasks generally performed by people who work in this job. This information comes from the O*NET database but, where necessary, has been edited to avoid exceeding 2,200 characters.

- **Career Cluster and Pathway:** This information cross-references the set of 16 career clusters developed by the U.S. Department of Education and used in various career information systems. Each cluster includes several career pathways that represent specializations. This information can help you identify jobs with education requirements that run parallel, at least through secondary school.

- **Personality Type:** The O*NET database assigns each job to its most closely related personality type. (For more on this topic, see the beginning of chapter 2.) The job descriptions include the name of the dominant personality type, plus perhaps one or two secondary personality types.

- **Skills:** Each job description includes the skills whose level-of-performance scores exceeded the average for all jobs by the greatest amount and whose ratings on the importance scale were higher than very low. You'll find as many as six such skills for each job, ranked them by the extent to which their rating exceeds the average. The skill names are defined in the next section of this appendix.

- **Education/Training Program(s):** This part of the job description provides the name of the educational or training program(s) for the job. It will help you identify sources of formal or informal training for a job that interests you.

- **Related Knowledge/Courses:** This entry can help you understand the most important knowledge areas that are required for a job and the types of courses or programs you will likely need to take to prepare for it. This information is derived from the O*NET database and shows, for each job, any knowledge area with a rating that was higher than the average rating for that knowledge area for all jobs. As many as six are listed in descending order. The terms are defined in the next section of this appendix.

Getting all the information we used in the job descriptions was not a simple process, and it is not always perfect. As in all matters involving career planning, use common sense in interpreting and applying the information.

Definitions of Terms Used in the Part II Descriptions

Definitions of Skills

Skill Name	Definition
Active Learning	Working with new material or information to grasp its implications.
Active Listening	Listening to what other people are saying and asking questions as appropriate.
Complex Problem Solving	Identifying complex problems, reviewing the options, and implementing solutions.
Coordination	Adjusting actions in relation to others' actions.
Critical Thinking	Using logic and analysis to identify the strengths and weaknesses of different approaches.
Cross-Functional Skills	These skills facilitate performance in a variety of job settings.
Equipment Maintenance	Performing routine maintenance and determining when and what kind of maintenance is needed.
Equipment Selection	Determining the kind of tools and equipment needed to do a job.
Installation	Installing equipment, machines, wiring, or programs to meet specifications.

Skill Name	Definition
Instructing	Teaching others how to do something.
Judgment and Decision Making	Weighing the relative costs and benefits of a potential action.
Learning Strategies	Using multiple approaches when learning or teaching new things.
Management of Financial Resources	Determining how money will be spent to get the work done and accounting for these expenditures.
Management of Material Resources	Obtaining and seeing to the appropriate use of equipment, facilities, and materials needed to do certain work.
Management of Personnel Resources	Motivating, developing, and directing people as they work; identifying the best people for the job.
Mathematics	Using mathematics to solve problems.
Monitoring	Assessing how well one is doing when learning or doing something.
Negotiation	Bringing others together and trying to reconcile differences.
Operation and Control	Controlling operations of equipment or systems.
Operation Monitoring	Watching gauges, dials, or other indicators to make sure a machine is working properly.
Operations Analysis	Analyzing needs and product requirements to create a design.
Persuasion	Persuading others to approach things differently.
Programming	Writing computer programs for various purposes.
Quality Control Analysis	Evaluating the quality or performance of products, services, or processes.
Reading Comprehension	Understanding written sentences and paragraphs in work-related documents.
Repairing	Repairing machines or systems, using the needed tools.
Science	Using scientific methods to solve problems.
Service Orientation	Actively looking for ways to help people.
Social Perceptiveness	Being aware of others' reactions and understanding why they react the way they do.

(continued)

(continued)

Skill Name	Definition
Speaking	Talking to others to effectively convey information.
Systems Analysis	Determining how a system should work and how changes will affect outcomes.
Systems Evaluation	Looking at many indicators of system performance and taking into account their accuracy.
Technology Design	Generating or adapting equipment and technology to serve user needs.
Time Management	Managing one's own time and the time of others.
Troubleshooting	Determining what is causing an operating error and deciding what to do about it.
Writing	Communicating effectively with others in writing as indicated by the needs of the audience.

Definitions of Knowledge/Courses

Knowledge/Course Name	Definition
Administration and Management	Principles and processes involved in business and organizational planning, coordination, and execution. This includes strategic planning, resource allocation, manpower modeling, leadership techniques, and production methods.
Biology	Plant and animal living tissue, cells, organisms, and entities, including their functions, interdependencies, and interactions with each other and the environment.
Building and Construction	Materials, methods, and the appropriate tools to construct objects, structures, and buildings.
Chemistry	Composition, structure, and properties of substances and of the chemical processes and transformations that they undergo. This includes uses of chemicals and their interactions, danger signs, production techniques, and disposal methods.
Clerical Studies	Administrative and clerical procedures and systems such as word-processing systems, filing and records management systems, stenography and transcription, forms, design principles, and other office procedures and terminology.

Knowledge/Course Name	Definition
Communications and Media	Media production, communication, and dissemination techniques and methods, including alternative ways to inform and entertain via written, oral, and visual media.
Computers and Electronics	Electric circuit boards, processors, chips, and computer hardware and software, including applications and programming.
Customer and Personal Service	Principles and processes for providing customer and personal services, including needs assessment techniques, quality service standards, alternative delivery systems, and customer satisfaction evaluation techniques.
Design	Design techniques, principles, tools, and instruments involved in the production and use of precision technical plans, blueprints, drawings, and models.
Economics and Accounting	Economic and accounting principles and practices, the financial markets, banking, and the analysis and reporting of financial data.
Education and Training	Instructional methods and training techniques, including curriculum design principles, learning theory, group and individual teaching techniques, design of individual development plans, and test design principles.
Engineering and Technology	Equipment, tools, and mechanical devices and their uses to produce motion, light, power, technology, and other applications.
English Language	Structure and content of the English language, including the meaning and spelling of words, rules of composition, and grammar.
Fine Arts	Theory and techniques required to produce, compose, and perform works of music, dance, visual arts, drama, and sculpture.
Food Production	Techniques and equipment for planting, growing, and harvesting of food for consumption, including crop rotation methods, animal husbandry, and food storage/handling techniques.

(continued)

(continued)

Knowledge/Course Name	Definition
Foreign Language	Structure and content of a foreign (non-English) language, including the meaning and spelling of words, rules of composition and grammar, and pronunciation.
Geography	Various methods for describing the location and distribution of land, sea, and air masses, including their physical locations, relationships, and characteristics.
History and Archeology	Past historical events and their causes, indicators, and impact on particular civilizations and cultures.
Law and Government	Laws, legal codes, court procedures, precedents, government regulations, executive orders, agency rules, and the democratic political process.
Mathematics	Numbers and their operations and interrelationships, including arithmetic, algebra, geometry, calculus, and statistics and their applications.
Mechanical Devices	Machines and tools, including their designs, uses, benefits, repair, and maintenance.
Medicine and Dentistry	Information and techniques needed to diagnose and treat injuries, diseases, and deformities. This includes symptoms, treatment alternatives, drug properties and interactions, and preventive health-care measures.
Personnel and Human Resources	Policies and practices involved in personnel/human resource functions. This includes recruitment, selection, training, and promotion regulations and procedures; compensation and benefits packages; labor relations and negotiation strategies; and personnel information systems.
Philosophy and Theology	Different philosophical systems and religions, including their basic principles, values, ethics, ways of thinking, customs, and practices and their impact on human culture.
Physics	Physical principles, laws, and applications, including air, water, material dynamics, light, atomic principles, heat, electric theory, earth formations, and meteorological and related natural phenomena.

Knowledge/Course Name	Definition
Production and Processing	Inputs, outputs, raw materials, waste, quality control, costs, and techniques for maximizing the manufacture and distribution of goods.
Psychology	Human behavior and performance, mental processes, psychological research methods, and the assessment and treatment of behavioral and affective disorders.
Public Safety and Security	Weaponry; public safety; security operations, rules, regulations, precautions, and prevention; and the protection of people, data, and property.
Sales and Marketing	Principles and methods involved in showing, promoting, and selling products or services. This includes marketing strategies and tactics, product demonstration and sales techniques, and sales control systems.
Sociology and Anthropology	Group behavior and dynamics; societal trends and influences; and cultures and their history, migrations, ethnicity, and origins.
Telecommunications	Transmission, broadcasting, switching, control, and operation of telecommunications systems.
Therapy and Counseling	Information and techniques needed to rehabilitate physical and mental ailments and to provide career guidance, including alternative treatments, rehabilitation equipment and its proper use, and methods to evaluate treatment effects.
Transportation	Principles and methods for moving people or goods by air, rail, sea, or road, including their relative costs, advantages, and limitations.

Where to Continue Your Career Exploration

This book should be only your first step in exploring a career. Here are some other resources and methods to use for continuing your career exploration:

- The *Occupational Outlook Handbook (OOH)* is America's best-selling career information resource. It features well-written, interesting descriptions for more than 300 major jobs in the U.S., plus summary information on additional jobs. The edition published by JIST includes exclusive information not found in the online version at www.bls.gov/oco.

- The O*NET database, online at http://online.onetcenter.org, contains a wealth of facts about occupations and is searchable by keywords, career clusters, industries, and several other characteristics. JIST publishes a print version, the *O*NET Dictionary of Occupational Titles*.

- Informational interviewing is a way to find out about an occupation from a person who actually holds the job. People are often happy to talk about their work, and the conversation can also help you to build your network. Make contact by using the procedures for cold calling discussed in chapters 4 and 5.

- Job shadowing means following a worker for a whole day at work, or at least a major chunk of time. If you're a student, your school may have job-shadowing programs arranged with local employers. If such a program is not available, you may be able to make arrangements through personal contacts or by talking to the human resources department of an employer. In some cases, insurance requirements or safety concerns may stand in your way. But if you do get an appointment, be sure to ask what style of clothing is appropriate (and then dress that way), show up on time, take notes on what you see and hear, and don't burden the worker with excessive questions and idle chatter (or the sound of your cell phone). Afterward, send a hand-written thank-you note, not an e-mail.

- An even better way to experience the work environment is to *do* work in it—as a volunteer, part-timer, or intern. You may not be able to do the same work as the occupation you're considering, but by working in the same setting you'll gain a better understanding of what the occupation is like.

Index

D

E

F–G

H

I

J

septic tank servicers and sewer pipe cleaners, 18, 44, 158–159

service orientation skills, 173

sewer pipe cleaners. *See* septic tank servicers and sewer pipe cleaners

sheriffs and deputy sheriffs, 20, 52, 159–160. *See also* police patrol officers

skills

definitions in descriptions, 172–174

learning as bridge to career goals, 54–56

SOC (Standard Occupational Classification), 168–170

social and human service assistants, 20, 160–161

social networking Web sites, 79–80

social perceptiveness skills, 173

Social personality type, 7, 15

matching with industries, 17

matching with jobs, 19

social workers. *See* child, family, and school social workers

sociology and anthropology knowledge/course, 177

software publishers job field, 31–33

speaking skills, 174

special assistance, except child day care job field, 29–30

special education teachers, preschool, kindergarten, and elementary school, 19, 30, 47, 161–162

speech-language pathologists, 19, 30, 38, 163–164

strategies for career goals, 5–6

survey researchers, 19, 36, 164–165

system analysis skills, 174

systems evaluation skills, 174

T

teachers and educators

education administrators, preschool and child care center/program, 19, 47, 109–110

kindergarten teachers, except special education, 19, 47, 125–126

preschool teachers, except special education, 19, 47, 147–148

self-enrichment education teachers, 19, 52, 157–158

special education teachers, preschool, kindergarten, and elementary school, 19, 30, 47, 161–162

technology design skills, 174

telecommunications equipment installers and repairers, except line installers, 18, 44, 165–166

telecommunications knowledge/course, 177

therapy and counseling knowledge/course, 177

Thomas Edison College Examination Program (TECEP), 56–57

time management skills, 174

training and development specialists, 19, 29–30, 50, 52, 166–167

Transition Assistance Office (military), 74

transportation knowledge/course, 177

troubleshooting skills, 174

Twitter, 79–80

The Twitter Job Search Guide, 80

U

U.S. Department of Education

authorized college credit by examination, 57

Classification of Instructional Programs, 168

Office of Vocational and Adult Education, 168

U.S. Department of Labor

Bureau of Labor Statistics, 168–170

Career Guide to Industries, 168

information accuracy, 168–169

Occupational Information Network (O*NET), 168–170, 178

V–Z

volunteering, 55, 69–70, 178

Whitcomb, Susan Britton, 80

workshops/single courses, 55, 70–71

writing skills, 174

Yellow Pages/Yellowbook.com, 80